KU-359-470

STANDPOINTS

MARRIAGE AND DIVORCE

STANDPOINTS

A Series of Discussions.

Edited by the Rev. K. E. KIRK, D.D.

1. MARRIAGE AND DIVORCE.
   By the Rev. K. E. Kirk, D.D.
2. GAMBLING.
   By the Rev. R. C. Mortimer, M.A.
3. EUGENICS.
   By the Rev. L. Hodgson, M.A., Hon. D.D., D.C.L.
4. SUPERSTITION.
   By the Rev. Herbert Thurston, S.J.
5. THE CHURCH AND POLITICS.
   By the Rev. C. S. Carpenter, M.A., B.D.

Other Volumes will appear shortly.

By DR. KIRK

Some Principles of Moral Theology, and their Application.

Ignorance, Faith and Conformity.

Conscience and its Problems.

The Vision of God.

The Threshold of Ethics.

MARRIAGE AND DIVORCE

By

K. E. KIRK

Cancelled from
Gladstone's Library

08 MAR 2023

THE CENTENARY PRESS
22 Suffolk Street, London, S.W.1

56635

MADE AND PRINTED BY
BUTLER AND TANNER LTD.
FROME AND LONDON

PUBLISHED IN MAY, 1933

ST. DEINIOL'S LIBRARY,
HAWARDEN.

EDITOR'S PREFACE

'STANDPOINTS,' the word which has been chosen as a general title for this series, is an accurate expression of its scope and purpose. The contributors share the common conviction that, in a time of intellectual and ethical uncertainty, nothing will more promote the cause of genuinely Christian progress than the frank expression of personal points of view, put forward as theses for discussion and criticism. It is by this dialectical process of question and answer, argument and counter-argument, and by this process alone, that the truth will ultimately be dissociated from the half-truths which surround it, and placed upon a secure foundation of its own.

With this end in view, no editorial compulsion of any kind has been exercised over the various writers. Each speaks for himself alone, committing neither his publisher, his editor, nor his fellow-contributors to the series, in any way whatever. What binds the writers together is simply the claim which each makes for himself, and allows for the others, that the 'standpoints' expressed are void of irrational bias and prejudice, and have been reached after serious enquiry, in which sympathetic attention has been given not least of all to the arguments of those schools of thought from which the writer has found himself in the end compelled to differ. If the same sympathetic attention is given by the reader to what is here written, the purpose of the series will have been secured.

K. E. KIRK.

OXFORD,
April, 1933.

INTRODUCTION

IT will be evident to the reader that this book is not a comprehensive treatment of the subjects mentioned in its title, but merely a discussion of some points of immediate practical interest at the present day. English readers have access already to two recent books of first-class importance by authors whose deaths have occasioned a sad loss to Anglican scholarship, Mr. O. D. Watkins' *Holy Matrimony*, and Canon Lacey's *Marriage in Church and State*. The first of these is an amazingly extensive collection and discussion of the original evidence for all periods of Christian history; its one defect is that occasionally the interpretation of the evidence is open to question, and leads to conclusions which are not beyond criticism. The second is written with all Canon Lacey's accustomed brilliance, and with a background of knowledge as deep as it is unobtrusive —so much so that the grounds on which its main positions are based may elude the less expert reader, and so lead him to regard it as more speculative than it really is. How fully I have made use of these two books, together with some of the best Continental authorities, should appear from

ST. DEINIOL'S LIBRARY,
HAWARDEN.

the footnotes ; but I should like to state explicitly that I am fully conscious of the degree in which I am indebted to them. Unfortunately for my purposes, Fr. G. H. Joyce's monumental and authoritative *Christian Marriage* appeared too late for me to refer to it more than once or twice.

I have to thank Canon J. S. Bezzant, Chancellor of Liverpool Cathedral, and G. R. Y. Radcliffe, Esq., Barrister-at-law, Fellow of New College and Principal of the Incorporated Law Society's School, for many suggestions and corrections which they communicated to me whilst kindly discharging the ungrateful task of reading the proofs.

K. E. K.

CONTENTS

MARRIAGE AND DIVORCE

I

MARRIAGE

I

CHRISTIAN moralists have not always approached the marriage question by the most felicitous route. They have frequently opened their argument with the outspoken challenge: "According to the Christian view, marriage is indissoluble." On examination, this challenge proves to be less formidable than at first appeared. It does not define 'marriage', and so leaves open the question whether there may not be other allowable sexual relationships between man and woman. And the word 'indissoluble' is ambiguous. It may of course mean that marriage '*ought* not to be dissolved'—which is the point at issue between the Christian tradition and its critics. But it may also mean that marriage '*cannot* be dissolved'—which seems to fly in the face of facts, and so provokes immediate scepticism on the whole question. It seems wiser, therefore, to examine the subject from a rather different angle.

On the Christian view, for a sex-union between man and woman to be according to God's will, it must fulfil certain conditions. What do we mean by 'according to God's will'? The phrase is one about which people are often apt to be confused. We may say at once that 'according to God's will' does not in the least mean the same as '*blameless* in God's sight'. All kinds of actions which are certainly 'contrary to God's will', or, more simply, 'wrong', may equally certainly be 'blameless', if the agent performs them in the full and conscientious conviction that they are right. It is 'wrong' of a mother to give way to all her children's whims and fancies; but if she knows no better (as we say), and conscientiously believes that it is right for her to do so, she is not to blame in the matter. So, too, in sexual relationships. There may be all kinds of unions among backward or uninstructed people which by reason of their ignorance we are entitled to call 'blameless'—polygamy, for example, among primitive tribes; or even more fortuitous matings than that. But their 'blamelessness' does not in any way whatever entitle us to say that they are according to the will of God.

Perhaps what we mean by 'according to God's will' can be expressed by the words, 'fulfilling God's highest ideal for man', or 'capable of forwarding God's purposes in the fullest degree'. The mother who spoils her children is not forwarding God's purposes for them to the extent to which they might be forwarded, nor is she fulfilling the ideal of perfect motherhood. Hence we call her action ' wrong ', however ' blameless ' we may recognize it to be. It is true that this distinction between the ' right ' and the ' blameless ' opens up many difficult problems which cannot be discussed here.[1] But the distinction is a necessary one if ethical discussion is to be kept on rational lines. Our business is to accept it as such, and then to ask, What are the necessary minimum conditions of a sexual union which is according to God's will—that is to say, which is capable of forwarding His purposes to the fullest extent?

On a certain number of these conditions all reasonable people will be agreed. In the first place, it is obvious that the union should not be a mere accidental relationship, but should be deliberate on both sides. This is often conveniently expressed by saying that it must be entered upon by means of a *contract*. In technical language, this is known as a contract *per verba de praesenti*—that is, one whose full implications come into force at the moment at which it is concluded, and not as from some future date. Thus the Prayer Book service has the explicit " I, N., take thee, N., to my wedded wife " (which must be *de praesenti*),

[1] I have dealt more fully with this extremely important and difficult question in a book called *The Threshold of Ethics*, ch. v.

in addition to the 'I will', which could refer to a *de futuro* contract alone. Furthermore, since the interests of the community at large are always vitally concerned in matters of sex, the contract must be implemented with such *forms* and *publicity*, and before such witnesses, as are required by the particular community or communities concerned, whether secular, or religious, or both.

The immediate purpose of the contract is, of course, the cohabitation of the contracting parties with a view to undertaking the responsibilities of parenthood, if children are born to them; and to securing 'the mutual society, help and comfort that the one ought to have of the other, both in prosperity and adversity'. It will clearly be one of the conditions of such a contract that both parties should *understand* its implications, and should *intend* to carry them out. Hence a lunatic cannot be a party to a valid marriage contract, since he cannot be supposed to understand it. Nor is a stage-marriage a valid marriage; for though the actor and actress may exchange vows before witnesses (and in some communities this in itself is all the publicity required), it is clear to all that they have no real intention of marrying one another, but are merely enacting their parts in the dramatist's play.

Again, it follows from the fact that both parties must intend to discharge the terms of the contract, that they must be *free agents*, and also *able* to perform the obligations they propose to undertake. 'Ability' depends mainly on physiological conditions; thus children are not physiologically able to undertake parenthood, nor are some adults. 'Free agency' is destroyed by any kind of coercion or compulsion; nor can a bridegroom strictly be called a free agent if, intending to contract a marriage with a certain lady, he finds that either by fraud or accident he has exchanged vows with someone else under the mistaken impression that she was his intended bride. The last two paragraphs can, in fact, conveniently be summarized by saying that in a true marriage there must be a *free and full consent of both parties*.

Another condition of the validity of a marriage contract is that the two parties must be *legally and morally competent* to enter into it. Almost all societies, however primitive and pagan, have recognized that there are certain natural or semi-natural relationships which make those between whom they exist legally or morally incompetent to enter into the sex-relationship as well. Such natural relationships are called relationships of *consanguinity* ('blood-ties', in fact);—examples are those of father and daughter, brother and sister. The semi-natural relationships are called *affinities*, and include those of a man with his wife's mother, and so forth. But there has been the greatest variety of opinion as to the list of such relationships which debar persons from entering into a valid sex-union; and even the Christian Church has not at all times nor in all places been of a single mind in the matter. The Lateran Council of 1215, for example, reduced the existing list considerably; the new Roman codex has introduced further simplifications. In English law, the Levitical prohibitions which were made binding by Henry VIII were amplified by Archbishop Parker's Table of 1563 (adopted in the canons of 1603), and this in turn was made statutory by Lord Lyndhurst's Act of 1835.

So far we have been dealing with conditions of a kind which everyone will recognize to be right and reasonable, unless—that is to say—he is an advocate of complete promiscuity in matters of sex. This does not mean that there may not be considerable divergences on points of detail; the agreement, in so far as it is achieved, is an agreement on principle alone. Now, however, we come to the final condition, and on this there is divergence not merely in matters of detail, but on the question of principle as well. According to the general Christian tradition, the contract must be a contract *between one man and one woman, to the exclusion of all others*, so long as they both shall live; and this condition—which prohibits anyone from going through the form of contract with a second partner during the lifetime of the first—must, like all the other primary conditions, be *understood* and *accepted* by both parties, if there is to be full and free consent. It is upon the truth or falsity of this last, and strictly Christian, condition that the whole problem of divorce hangs; for it is by virtue of this condition that the Church speaks of marriage as 'indissoluble'.

II

These, then, according to the Christian view, are the necessary minimum conditions of a union which shall be capable of realizing God's full purposes in the matter of sex. Where all these conditions are present, and the contract is entered into in accordance with them, Christianity says that a 'marriage' has taken place; and the parties to the contract are said to be 'married', or 'husband and wife'. Where, furthermore, the parties are both of them baptized persons, the marriage is called a 'Christian marriage'. According to age-long tradition, 'Christian marriage' is further said to be a 'sacrament'—which we may understand to mean that it brings with it not merely moral obligations and natural joys, but also supernatural grace to sanctify the joys and strengthen the recipients for the discharge of their obligations. But before proceeding to consider the doctrine of Christian marriage, there are one or two observations that must be made on the subject of the conditions we have been considering.

First of all, although we may expect general agreement on the principles underlying most of the conditions we have reviewed, there is bound to be (as we have said) a vast amount of discussion on the details. Indeed, even within the confines of Christian and western civilization, their intricacies have exercised the ingenuity of casuists, canonists, and civil lawyers, from time immemorial. Among the obvious questions which present themselves are these :—What evidence is necessary to prove defective consent, or coercion, or defective understanding of the implications of marriage ? What is the age at which children may be considered physiologically able to mate ? What are the degrees of consanguinity and affinity within which matrimony is contrary to the will of God ?—and so forth. Details such as these would probably not interest the general reader, and are in any case beyond the scope of this book. One or two of them we must allude to at a later stage ; but the fact that there are so many, and that the questions they raise are so complicated, will suffice to show that our subject is one which cannot be dealt with fully without a formidable equipment of technical knowledge.

Again, the conditions enumerated above are at best only the *necessary minimum conditions* without which (according to the Christian view) a union cannot be regarded as in accordance with the will of God. It is obvious, therefore, that the mere presence of these conditions alone does not necessarily imply that the marriage will fulfil

God's purposes for it. Though all the conditions mentioned were observed, the marriage might still be 'enterprised and taken in hand unadvisedly, lightly, or wantonly'; in such a case it has little chance of pleasing God. Or, again, mutual distrust, incompatibility of temper or temperament, estrangement or friction may creep in at a later stage, and prevent the marriage from being what it ought to be. All we have said is that, where the conditions enumerated above are not present, there we have a union which (blameless and even beautiful in many respects though it may be) is of such a nature as perhaps to impede rather than to forward God's ultimate purposes. The ground is not clear for a successful advance to the ideal, such as is at all events possible where the conditions have been observed.

It is to be noticed, further, that, according to the general Christian view, the moment at which the marriage 'begins' (if we may use this phrase) is the moment at which the contract is made, and not the moment at which the union is consummated between husband and wife. That comes afterwards; it must be the intention of the pair that it should come, but it is not of the essence of matrimony.[1] This principle, which the Church

[1] This is generally agreed to-day; but O. D. Watkins stands for the other view—see his *Holy Matrimony*, pp. 112–35; and for the evidence, A. Esmein, *Le Mariage en Droit Canonique* [2], i, pp. 102–7.

took over from Roman law, will not affect our discussion very much. What we have rather to notice is that, though there is general unanimity on the point, there is also a certain agreement that non-consummated marriage is to some extent less formally complete than consummated union. The point is one to which we must recur on a later page.[1]

Finally, it will of course have been observed that we have made no attempt to establish the truth of the last and all-important condition—that of the indissolubility of marriage. But we have at least cleared up some of the difficulties surrounding these ambiguous words. What is meant when Christians speak of marriage as ' indissoluble ' is that no one is acting in accordance with the will of God (however ' blameless ' he may be in the matter) who enters into a contract of union intending at some later stage to disown it, or reserving to himself the right to disown it in certain events or contingencies. Nor is it according to that same will of God that any person should attempt to enter into a second marriage contract during the lifetime of a partner with whom he has already made such a contract. But to prove the truth of this position, in face of the doubts of the modern world, is no easy task ; what is to be said about it we will try to say in the fourth chapter of this book.

[1] *Infra*, p. 74.

III

Few communities, whether civilized or uncivilized, religious or secular, have failed to recognize that the sex relationship is a matter of public interest; hence churches and states have almost always attempted to regulate it by legislation. In so doing, they have been compelled to face those problems of detail to which we have already alluded, and to reach conclusions upon them. One such conclusion of the canon law had a far-reaching influence upon the Christian theory of marriage. The question might be raised :—Where two parties have apparently entered into a marriage contract with one another, how far may it be assumed that they genuinely intended 'marriage' in the lifelong, indissoluble sense? At first sight the matter was not a difficult one. On the general principle that a man must always be treated as innocent until he is proved guilty, or that a suspected offender must always receive the benefit of the doubt, canonists held that the intention to contract lawful marriage must always be presumed unless and until the contrary were proved beyond all possibility of question.[1]

[1] A. Esmein, *op. cit.* (1929), i, pp. 198, 336–41; cp. generally on this E. J. Mahoney, 'Matrimonial Consent and Divorce,' in *The Clergy Review*, vol. i, no. 1 (Jan. 1931), pp. 26 ff. For a recent example of the same principle in English matrimonial procedure, see Nachimson *v.* Nachimson, *L.R.* (1930), Prob., pp. 85–99, 217–46.

This conclusion is no doubt acceptable enough when applied to a community in which the full Christian view of matrimony is known to and accepted by all and sundry. But at an early date the Church took the daring step of applying it also to the heathen world, and assuming that there also, despite appearances to the contrary, any marriage contract, duly solemnized according to the accepted ceremonies of the tribe or nation concerned, was a contract intended to bind one man to one woman, to the exclusion of all others, during the lifetime of them both. Thus if a married heathen or Jewish couple presented themselves together for baptism, no new marriage vows were required between them. Their non-Christian marriage contract was a true marriage contract, and its validity was carried on into their new Christian condition. And on the other hand, if a heathen couple had been 'divorced' by secular authority, and contracted second alliances with new partners, they might not cohabit with these second partners after baptism. The indissoluble bond created by their first marriage still held them, so long as there was no definite and convincing proof that they never intended it to do so. So, in S. Augustine's day, 'baptism was refused to men who had put away their wives and married others (whom they refused to give up), and to women who had put away their husbands and married others; since our Lord beyond all doubt testifies such (second) unions to be not marriages but adulteries '.[1]

These facts are of great importance. They prove how tenaciously the Church held to the idea of indissolubility as a necessary condition for a true marriage. But the matter was not by any means so simple as the last paragraph has suggested. The principle of the universal indissolubility of the marriage contract was crossed by another, and very curious one. This is the strange permission given by S. Paul in 1 Corinthians 7 [12-15] (commonly called the 'Pauline privilege'), whereby if one of two married heathen asked for baptism (the other remaining unbaptized) he or she was entitled on certain conditions to disown the heathen partner and marry a Christian.[2] The conditions in question go back to that laid down by S. Paul—the heathen partner must be 'unwilling to abide' with the Christian partner. What exactly constituted 'unwillingness', and how the fact was to be established, constituted a difficult problem, and gave rise to innumerable canonical discussions as complex as they are interesting.

[1] Augustine, *De fid. et op.*, 2; cp. *De conj. adult.*, i. 28. For doubts on this point contrast Prümmer, *Manuale Theol. Mor.* (1915), vol. iii, § 650, with § 679, n. 4. Many authorities suggest that S. Augustine contradicts himself, but this does not emerge from careful study of the passages in question.

[2] S. Paul does not confer the right to remarry in so many words; but in spite of the dissent of S. Augustine (*De conj. adult.*, i. 25) and Canon Lacey (*Marriage in Church and State*, p. 19), it seems the inevitable inference.

But they do not affect our immediate purpose, and therefore may safely be left on one side.

It must be confessed at once that this 'Pauline privilege' stands on no recognizable basis of principle, and has caused the greatest possible confusion among canonists. Nevertheless, it had the full authority of Scripture, and the Church on that account found herself incapable of ignoring it. Some of the most ingenious decisions in the history of the Christian marriage law spring from the simultaneous application of the Pauline privilege and of the principle of the natural indissolubility of heathen marriage, particularly in the case of the conversion of polygamists.

It was held, for example, that a converted polygamist must retain the first wife of his unconverted state, if she were baptized with him, dismissing the others, whether they also agreed to be baptized or not.[1] On the theory we are considering, this ruling is natural enough. The first marriage was a true marriage, even in heathendom; it was, moreover, the only true marriage, the remainder being concubinous. If, however, the first wife refused to be baptized, several courses were open to the converted husband. She was his true wife, therefore he was at liberty, and indeed was encouraged, to retain her. On the other hand, by virtue of the Pauline privilege, he

[1] Aquinas, *S.T.*, Suppl., q. 59, a. 3, ad 4; Paul III, Const. *Altitudo* (A.D. 1537); Benedict XIV, *de Syn. Dioc.*, xiii. 21. 2.

might dismiss her, at all events if she was 'unwilling to abide peaceably'. In this case he was free, of course, to take as his Christian wife any other of his 'wives' who might choose to be baptized with him [1]—or indeed any other Christian woman—*but he must enter into a formal marriage contract with her.*[2] The reason is clear. To none of his 'wives' except the first had he any conjugal duty at all. If he dismissed the first on the basis of the Pauline privilege, he was free to marry one of the others; but only by a new contract, not by virtue of any relationship existing between them in the preceding polygamous state.

A further complication was produced by the fact that sometimes the polygamist professed himself unable to remember which of his wives he had married first. If we assume the *bona fides* of such a state of mind, the ecclesiastical solution once again follows a line of sound principle. The mere fact of the husband's inability to remember which of his so-called wives he married first is evidence

[1] Pius V, Const. *Romani Pontificis* (A.D. 1571). If none of the wives would be converted, and the first would not abide peaceably, he must abandon them all; though he might ask for a dispensation from the impediment of *disparitas cultus* in order to marry any one of them he chose; Prümmer, iii. § 679, n. 9 (from *Coll. de Prop. Fide*, n. 1045).

[2] This is not explicitly stated by Pius V; but Benedict XIV rightly insists that it must be read into the ruling (unless the latter is to be wholly irregular), and enacts that it shall be explicitly required in all future cases (*de Syn. Dioc.*, xiii. 21. 6, 7, 8). Cp. Aquinas, *loc. cit.*

that no relationship worthy of the name of marriage has ever existed at all between him and the women of his household. Their condition was one of chaotic promiscuity alone. Consequently he has conjugal obligations towards none of the ladies. He is free to marry any one of them who will be baptized with him; but—once again—*there must be a marriage ceremony*, since hitherto they have not been united in anything that can be called wedlock.[1]

The illustrations will suffice to show how rigidly the Church has held to the principle of the 'natural indissolubility of marriage'—the principle, that is, that the marriage vows of non-Christians to one another must be presumed to imply the same intention of lifelong fidelity as the Christian ceremony, unless clear and convincing evidence to the contrary can be cited. No doubt heathen 'marriages' were often scrutinized and found to be *de facto* null and void [2] because of some defect in the original conditions; but *de jure* they were as indissoluble as Christian ones. Other illustrations could easily be quoted. Thus some authorities, among them S. Augustine,[3] held the heathen marriage tie to be so permanent and

[1] Paul III, Const. *Altitudo* (A.D. 1537). Here the marriage contract is explicitly required—a fact which Watkins (p. 561) entirely overlooks; attributing, in consequence, to Paul a view which he never held.

[2] See *infra*, pp. 49, 75 ff., on nullity.

[3] *Supra*, p. 23, n. 1.

sacred that they rejected the interpretation of the Pauline privilege as a permission to marry a second partner; and regarded it as a permission to *separate* from the heathen partner alone, without the right of remarriage during his or her lifetime. Others restricted the occasions on which the 'privilege' might be enjoyed so severely as to make it virtually inoperative; and so by another method secured that in practice the heathen union should be treated as permanently binding when either of the partners came to be baptized. We may attribute these tendencies on the part of the Church to an incurable optimism, or to a perverse obstinacy, or to a large-hearted charity, as we will. But whatever the motive was, its outcome is manifest—Christian theologians all assumed without hesitation that the heathen in general were sufficiently acquainted with God's purposes in 'instituting matrimony', to entitle and require their contracts to be regarded as indissoluble in intention.

The technical expression of this view is to be found in the sentence, "Marriage is indissoluble by natural law,"[1]—for of the first principles, at all events, of the law of nature, the heathen were never supposed to be ignorant. It is true that another view has often been put forward by Chris-

[1] E.g. *Conc. Trid.*, sess. xxiv, *doctrina de sacr. matr.*, Denz.-Bannw., *Enchiridion*, 968–70; Benedict XIV, Const. *Dei miseratione* (1741); Pius IX, *Syllabus*, 67 (Denz.-Bannw., 1767); Leo XIII, Encycl. *Arcanum* (1880) (Denz.-Bannw., 1853, 1854), etc.

tian theologians—the view that "the indissolubility of marriage derives from its sacramental character".[1] Now sacraments exist only within the Christian Church; and consequently this second view implies that the obligation of indissolubility binds only in the case of Christian wedlock, and has no force where a union is contracted between unbaptized persons. The logical corollary would of course be that when a heathen comes forward for baptism, no enquiry into his previous matrimonial relationships is necessary, since he has never been 'married' in the Christian sense of the word at all. And although he would certainly be free to marry any baptized person who caught his fancy, it is doubtful whether he would be allowed to retain an unbaptized partner if he wished to do so. For he would have to go through a ceremony of genuine marriage with her, and this would be tantamount to marrying a heathen—a practice which the Church has always deprecated most strongly.

These logical corollaries of the view that the indissolubility of marriage derives from its sacramental character were never put into effect. They would have been flat violations of the general Pauline position, which encouraged the baptized convert, as the usual course, to retain his heathen

[1] For this view, which is held by O. D. Watkins, and strenuously opposed by Canon Lacey, see A. Esmein, *op. cit.*, i, pp. 68–71.

partner [1]; and of the ruling of some of the principal Fathers of the Church, who *required* the heathen partner to be retained if he or she were willing to 'abide peaceably'.[2] We must regard the 'view' in question, therefore, as a popular rather than a strictly theological statement. Perhaps it means no more than that many heathen 'marriages' do not *de facto* involve a contract of lifelong fidelity. Perhaps, again, it is simply an expression of the supreme dignity of Christian marriage as a sacrament; [3] or a metaphor to express the sanctity of the marriage vow in general.[4] At all events, it cannot by any possible exercise of dexterity be made to fit the Church's practice in the matter of married heathen who asked for baptism. Our general impression of the emphasis laid by Christianity on the indissolubility of the marriage bond—an emphasis shown by its extension of this principle to the whole of the heathen world—remains unimpaired.

[1] 1 Cor. 7 [12, 13].

[2] Watkins, pp. 460, 497, 499–501; cp. 534, 556.

[3] The Augustinian passages usually quoted to show that the indissolubility of marriage depends upon its sacramental character (*De nupt. et con.*, i. 10, 13, 17, 21; *De bon. conj.*, i. 7, 8, 15, 24; *De fid. et op.*, 7, etc.) either reflect this point of view, or merely contrast the Christian law with the *secular* laws of non-Christian societies.

[4] So several mediaeval authorities expressly use the word 'sacrament' of heathen marriages; Honorius III, c. 11, X. i, 36; Innocent III, c. 8, X. iv, 19; Boniface VIII, c. 1, *Sext.*, iii, 15; Aquinas, *S.T.*, Suppl., q. 59, a. 2, ad 1.

IV

Among the conditions requisite for a true marriage in the sight of God we noticed that of *due publicity*. Here, again, is a question which has provoked intense and varied discussion, and has swayed the course of ecclesiastical history. The degree of publicity required by the codes of different Christian bodies ranges from no witnesses at all, as in Scots law,[1] to a formal exchange of vows in *facie ecclesiae*, as with the Council of Trent. The matter cannot, however, be dismissed without further discussion, for on it turn some very important questions concerned with the present marriage law in England.

Clandestine marriages were one of the banes of the middle ages. The vows were exchanged in all kinds of circumstances and with every degree of informality. The result was that on this account alone (not to mention many others) [2] few could be certain that their union might not ultimately be declared invalid. A remedy—at all events a partial remedy [3]—was obvious; the Church had foreseen it from the earliest days. Whatever else might change, the ecclesiastical hierarchy was

[1] *E. Br.*[11] xvii, p. 758.

[2] *Infra*, p. 86.

[3] For the scandal of the Fleet marriages, and similar irregularities, enabled the purpose of the provision to be easily evaded (Lacey, pp. 189, 190).

relatively permanent. If, then, all marriages were celebrated before a priest, there would be some guarantee of stability. The Church did not indeed for many centuries insist that marriage contracts made in the absence of a priest were null and void.[1] Her efforts were directed solely to secure that a priest should habitually be present; and this not merely to avoid clandestinity, but also to secure the highly desirable end that the marriage should receive the blessing of the Church at the earliest possible moment.

But at length a new position came to be accepted. For the Roman communion, the Council of Trent laid down that the presence of a priest was necessary for a valid marriage. In England the process was slower, and by a curious combination of circumstances the initiative was taken by the State rather than the Church. But the result was the same. In 1753, Lord Hardwicke's Act declared that all marriages (other than those of Jews and Quakers), not contracted in the parish church of one of the parties, and before an ordained minister and with his active participation, should be 'null and void' to all intents and purposes whatsoever. It is only fair to add, with Canon Lacey, that "churchmen did more than acquiesce" in this legislation; "they took an active part in promoting the measure,

[1] See the important references in Phillimore, *Ecclesiastical Law*, p. 552; and generally, Esmein, i, pp. 116–18, 198–203; Pollock and Maitland, *History of English Law*, ii, pp. 368 ff.

and their own courts enforced its provisions with rigour ".[1]

For a period, then, English law adopted the principle which has been the 'prevalent doctrine' of the Greek Church 'for centuries',[2] and the official rule of the Roman Church since Trent—that no marriage is valid unless it is celebrated in church by an accredited minister of the Church. But it was only for a period. The civil legislation of the nineteenth century made marriage valid in England if celebrated, after due notice and in the presence of witnesses, before the registrar—a purely secular official.[3] The purpose of this legislation, of course, was to satisfy the conscientious scruples of non-conformists and non-Christians; but it had a curious and important result for Churchmen. The Church, no doubt, could have rejected the new development, and insisted that for her own members, at all events, only marriage before a priest would be held valid. So far, however, from taking this course, which would undoubtedly have involved a clash with the State, the Church acquiesced (though with some reluctance) in the new situation. No violation of principle was involved. The circumstances were wholly different from those of

[1] Lacey, p. 193.

[2] See Watkins, p. 91; but it was not an official rule prior to the eighth century at earliest (*ib.*, p. 100).

[3] The Act of 1836; by the Act of 1898, marriage may be solemnized by the minister of any regular place of worship certified by the Registrar-General, in such place of worship.

the middle ages. A settled government meant that marriage contracts could be registered as safely with the civil as with the ecclesiastical official; whilst the right of the Church to insist on the propriety of a marriage between Christians receiving the blessing of the Church was maintained by a later provision that the full marriage service might be read over the parties, if so desired, at any time after the marriage before the registrar, provided that nothing was said or done to suggest in any way that the civil formality had not constituted a valid marriage.

But this acquiescence of the Church in the new state of things, while involving no sacrifice of principle, did as a matter of fact bring to light another traditional principle which had been in danger of obsolescence. It was the principle that the essence of marriage, as regards its form, consists in the exchange of vows before accredited witnesses, not in the presence or words of a priest as such, nor in the blessing of the Church. Various phrases in the rituals ("We are gathered together in the sight of God and in the face of this congregation to *join together* this man and this woman," in the English office, and still more "Ego conjungo vos", in the Roman) had obscured this truth, and incidentally had confirmed the inaccurate and ambiguous view that the indissolubility of marriage depended upon its sacramental (i.e. religious) character. But no sooner was it admitted that marriage before a registrar was true marriage, and in no way debarred from communion, than the primitive and Catholic doctrine was established once more.

V

The importance of this fact for modern discussions cannot be over-estimated. It is very often suggested that register office marriages are in some sense or other less binding than marriage in church. Two grounds may be adduced for this opinion. The first is that the register office vows are of a less solemn and explicit character than those of the Prayer Book, and in particular do not contain the phrase " till death us do part ". But to this it can be replied that the ceremony before the registrar is required to include the all-important contract *per verba de praesenti*, in the words " I . . . take thee . . . to my (lawful) wedded wife (or husband) ". And if it be said that this does not appear in itself to imply the condition of a life-long indissoluble partnership, the answer is equally clear. English law knows only one kind of ' marriage ', and that is " the voluntary union for life of one man with one woman to the exclusion of all others ".[1] How this judicial definition is reconciled in English law with the fact that divorce and remarriage during the lifetime of the first partner have been legal since 1857, is a matter for the lawyer, and not for the theologian, to explain.

[1] Halsbury, *Laws of England*, xvi, p. 278, with references there.

This, however, raises the second argument. English law, it is said—the law which established the register office marriage—has also established or allowed 'divorce' with the right to remarry. Hence the register office marriage cannot, in law, abrogate the right of the partners to claim a divorce from one another in certain possible circumstances. Here, however, we must be clear as to what is the point in dispute. All that matters, at this stage, is to insist that in principle register office marriages stand on exactly the same footing, as far as baptized persons are concerned, as marriages in church. And this, it may be confidently asserted, is a point on which Church and State are absolutely agreed. The State, on its side, allows 'divorce',[1] in specified circumstances, without making the slightest differentiation between marriages which have taken place in church and marriages which have taken place in register offices. The Church, in accordance with Catholic principle, accepts the register office marriage between baptized persons as in every sense a full Christian marriage; and in so far as it refuses divorce to married Christians, makes no differentiation between the case in which they have contracted before a registrar and the case in which they have contracted before a priest.

Thus both State and Church are agreed that there

[1] In the remainder of this chapter, 'divorce' has its customary modern meaning of divorce with the right to a second marriage during the lifetime of the first partner. See pp. 47, 48.

are only two kinds of sex-relationship in which a man and a woman can stand to one another—either they are married, or they are not. To suggest that *three* relationships are possible—e.g. marriage *without* the right to divorce (marriage in church, let us say), marriage *with* the right to divorce (marriage before a registrar), and no marriage at all—is to suggest something of which neither Church nor State has ever heard; something moreover which the Church could not for a moment admit without rewriting the whole of her carefully thought-out teaching upon the subject of sex. Either the full vows have been exchanged in due form, and then there is a marriage; or they have not, and then (whatever may happen afterwards),[1] there is none.

But it may be said: "In view of *both* the arguments suggested—the permission of divorce given by the same State which has instituted the register office marriage, and the absence of the words 'till death us do part' from the latter ceremony—it is more than likely that persons contracting before a registrar will hold themselves free to seek divorce if at a later stage either gives the other occasion for it. And this is tantamount to saying that, in all probability, they will not be consenting to a Christian union at all." It must frankly be admitted that there is some ground for this suggestion; and it is no very satisfactory answer to say that in view of the general ignorance and scepticism about

[1] *Infra*, pp. 81–4.

Christian principles in this, as in other matters, which prevail in England to-day, it is very probable that many who contract in church do so with the same reservation. The best that can be said is that, for the present at all events, parties who contract in a register office are presumed to have done so with the implication of indissolubility, as in good canon law they should be,[1] equally with parties who contract in church; and that there is not as yet any conclusive evidence that this principle is no longer applicable.

But a time may come when the laws of Church and State will have diverged so far from one another that it will be morally impossible to assume that those who contract by a purely civil ceremony have in any way understood, or assented to, the implication of indissolubility. If such a time comes, the Church will not indeed have the right to insist that a State, of which many members do not accept the Christian tradition, should force them to conform to it in this respect.[2] But she will be free to declare that a register office marriage is not a valid marriage-contract so far as Christians are concerned. The strict logic of this situation would seem to require that she should excommunicate all Christians living together as husband and wife who have contracted by the civil ceremony

[1] *Supra*, p. 21.

[2] Cp. Lacey, p. 223; J. N. Figgis, *Churches in the Modern State*, pp. 120–5.

alone. For (once again) there seems to be no *tertium genus*. A man or a woman are either married to one another 'according to God's holy ordinance', or they are not; and if they are not, and yet cohabit, they would seem to be debarred from receiving the sacraments. Whether there is any escape from this dilemma, we will consider at a later stage.[1]

VI

In the meantime we may glance at one further point. It is sometimes suggested that the difficulties which already exist, because of the divergence of ecclesiastical and civil law in this matter of divorce, would be mitigated if 'universal civil marriage' were established in England. The legislation necessary to bring about this result would presumably provide that all persons desiring to be regarded as married in the eyes of the State must contract before a registrar; and as far as the State were concerned, it would be a matter of indifference whether a marriage service were performed thereafter for them in church or not. Indeed, the religious ceremony might even take place *before* the civil ceremony; for once it was clearly recognized that civil marriage did not connote religious marriage, and *vice versâ*, the order in which the two ceremonies took place would not matter.

[1] *Infra*, p. 137, n.

It is difficult to see that any direct practical result would be achieved by putting this suggestion into effect. The authorities of the Church would still have to decide, as they have to decide to-day, whether the civil 'marriage' involved such an implication of indissolubility as to entitle it to be regarded as a genuine marriage in the Christian sense. If they held (as they appear to hold at present) that it could be so regarded, they might of course require all Christian couples, *as a matter of Church order*, to have their marriages blessed at a formal ecclesiastical service. But they could not reasonably insist, any more than at present, that the parties must, *as a condition of a valid Christian marriage*, contract in church as well as in the register office. Such a requirement would not indeed be absolutely illegitimate in strict canon law, since it might be held that the parties' intention to contract ought to be notified specifically to the Church to which they belong, as well as to the State. But it would be definitely provocative, if the vows before the registrar were held to imply the condition of indissolubility; for the main purpose of marriage *in facie ecclesiae* has always been to secure that there is full consent before witnesses to an indissoluble contract—a purpose which, on this hypothesis, the register office marriage would sufficiently secure.

If, on the other hand, the Church held that the civil marriage, by reason of an increasing laxity of the State in the matter of divorce, could no longer be regarded as true marriage in the sight of God, she would have to decide the canonical status of baptized persons who contracted before the registrar but failed to contract in church; and so would be in no better case than she may still find herself (as was suggested in the last paragraph) under the present system. In either case, no immediate advantage could be expected from the universalization of civil marriage. Something, however, might perhaps be gained indirectly. As things stand at present in this country, *some* religious marriages are recognized by the State as supplying all that is required for a civil marriage. Under the proposed system, *no* religious marriage would any longer have any effect in civil law. This would at least suggest to the world at large that civil marriage and religious marriage may have entirely different purposes—the purpose of the former being merely to secure certain legal rights and obligations to the contracting parties; the purpose of the latter, to secure that men and women should unite according to the will of God. This would imply that, just as religious marriage can only discharge the purpose of civil marriage if the State legislates to that effect, so civil marriage can only discharge the purpose of religious marriage, if the Church decides to recognize it as valid. Thus the moment the State enacted that all citizens, to secure the legal ends of civil marriage, must contract before a registrar, whether there were a service in church as well or not, it would become clear that the Church had an equal right to require her members to contract in ecclesiastical form, in order that God's purposes for their marriage might be recognized.

The consequences of this would be far-reaching. It would still, of course, be open to the Church (as at present) to acknowledge the civil contract as an adequate guarantee of the publicity, and even of the intention to contract indissolubly, requisite for a valid religious marriage. And in any case, in so far as she recognized that human ordinances have a real claim upon the loyalty of citizens, she ought at least to insist that she would regard no one as ecclesiastically married, who did not also contract according to the secular laws in force for the time being.[1]

But if at the same time she required that all those who claimed the privileges of Church membership must be married by a religious ceremony as well as a civil one, and that not merely as a matter of propriety, but as a condition of their marriage being regarded as a valid religious marriage; and insisted furthermore that not all those whom the State allowed to contract civilly would necessarily be regarded as competent to contract ecclesiastically as well; these demands might meet with a more favourable hearing than they are likely to receive under the present system. For the idea that the

[1] This rather obvious consideration eliminates some of the possibilities foreshadowed by Lacey, *op. cit.*, pp. 207, 208.

civil and religious marriages respectively do not necessarily bring about each other's purposes would already be in the air; and it would be more generally recognized than it is at present that the Church has a right to an independent discipline over her own members in the matter of marriage. Hence, though the institution of universal civil marriage will in no sense provide any immediate practical solution of our present difficulties, it might at least create in time an atmosphere favourable to the only kind of solution which a Christian could accept.

II

DIVORCE

I

THE doctrine of the indissolubility of marriage was very much a novelty in the world into which Christianity brought it. Despite the protest of prophets,[1] it was the accepted view, among all but the strictest sect of Jews, that a man could divorce his wife and marry another for grounds of varying degrees of triviality—'if she let the broth burn', for example, or if he found another woman more beautiful[2]; whilst a slave-wife, at all events, from whom a husband withheld food, raiment, or cohabitation, was free to leave him and find a new husband elsewhere.[3] In the Roman world even laxer customs prevailed, whereby, to all intents and purposes, either partner might divorce the other on the slightest pretext, and marry again; the law intervening only to regulate the practice, and to secure that grave injustice was

[1] E.g. Mal. 2 [16].

[2] So, for example, Hillel–Watkins, p. 52; and cp. on the Hillel–Shammai controversy, *infra*, pp. 59, ff.

[3] Ex. 21 [10, 11].

not done in the distribution of the dowry and estate.[1]

Thus, apart from all question of the weakness of the flesh, the new Christian doctrine ran counter to the whole tenour of contemporary practice. That it survived in its full rigour as long as it did is a fact in itself remarkable. It is true that, during the ascetic primitive centuries, it had a safeguard, or protective outwork, in the marked tendency on the part of the Church to discourage, if not to prohibit, second marriages of any kind whatever. But this was an innovation even more startling than the former; and the tenacity with which the Church held to both doctrines is one of the most striking proofs imaginable of the strength of her corporate self-consciousness in opposition to the massed forces of a disapproving and menacing environment. But the system was too rigorous to endure. Flesh and blood demanded an outlet, loophole, or safety-valve.

By the beginning of the third century there is evidence that women, who for one reason or another had left their first partners, were marrying others during the lifetime of their original husbands; and what women were doing, we can scarcely doubt that men were doing too. It is true that Tertullian's statement to this effect does not put it beyond question that he is referring only to the exercise of the Pauline privilege; for

[1] Watkins, p. 193.

he is primarily concerned only with discountenancing second marriages in general.[1] But his contemporary, Origen, makes the matter quite clear. In Egypt, at all events, not only were women who had secured a divorce remarrying during the lifetime of their original husbands, but some of the rulers of the Church were sanctioning the practice.[2] A century later the matter has become so serious that canons and councils are legislating against it.[3] And with the great invasion of the Church by the semi-heathen world which was the inevitable sequel of the conversion of Constantine, it became clear once and for all that the existing ecclesiastical practice in the matter was too severe to be retained in all its stark integrity.

From that time forward, no branch of the Christian Church (except as we shall see, the modern Church of England) has been without some recog-

[1] Tert., *ad ux.*, ii. 1—"*Women who, where by divorce or by a husband's death*, an opportunity was offered to them, had not only thrown it away, but had also forgotten the precept that they should marry only in the Lord." His primary interest, therefore, is to prevent second marriages; his secondary interest to prevent the marriage of Christians with heathen. The problem of the remarriage of a Christian who has obtained a divorce from a Christian partner is not considered as such.

[2] *Comm. in Mt.* xix—the passage cited at length, Watkins, pp. 186–8. Watkins (p. 214) regards this as perhaps an instance of the Pauline privilege. But this is impossible, since Origen expressly condemns it as 'contrary to Scripture', which the Pauline privilege is not.

[3] *Ap. Can.* 47; Elvira (A.D. 306), cc. 8, 9; Arles (314), c. 10.

nized loophole or safety-valve. Here, however, we must begin by drawing as clear a distinction as possible between three terms—the terms *separation*, *divorce*, and *nullity*—all of them relevant to our purposes.

By 'separation' is meant 'separation from bed and board'—*divortium a mensa et thoro* or *quoad thorum et cohabitationem*. In all normal circumstances, of course, husband and wife are required by Christian law to live together, and to discharge their mutual obligations towards one another. But for exceptional reasons, they are on occasion allowed to live separate lives—sometimes for a time only (where, for example, the man's business or vocation requires it); sometimes permanently, where, for example, cohabitation is manifestly morally impossible owing to the cruelty of one partner towards the other, incompatibility of temper or some other grave and urgent cause.[1] The partners are not entitled, therefore, to separate by mutual consent on any grounds of mere inconvenience; and in principle *permanent* separation is only allowable, in canon law, by virtue of an official decision of a Church court.[2] Nevertheless, even where this rule is in force, the persons concerned are allowed to obtain a judicial separation from a

[1] Cp. *Conc. Trid.*, sess. xxiv, can. 8 de matr. (Denz.-Bannw., n. 978).

[2] Aquinas, *Summa Theol.*, Suppl., q. 62, a. 3. But see c. 4, X. iv. 19; c. 9, X. iv. 1; Prümmer, iii, p. 485—an exception is admitted in cases of open and notorious adultery.

civil court as well, in order that the legal questions arising out of the readjustment of their relationship may be settled in due and binding form.[1] In rare cases, a civil decree of divorce may be obtained if the same ends can be secured in no other way.[2] It is needless to add that 'separation' does not carry with it any right of remarriage to other partners during the lifetime of the separated couple.

'Divorce' (*divortium a vinculo*) is commonly used of the dissolution of a valid marriage by legitimate authority, conferring the right of remarriage with a new partner, during the lifetime of the former partner, on each of the divorced persons. Here we find ourselves at once in the midst of controversy. It is the consistent theory of the western Church that no human authority can dissolve a marriage once validly contracted.[3] According to Canon Lacey, the same is the case with the eastern Church.[4] In the cases where permission is given by that Church to a person to marry a new partner during the lifetime of a divorced husband or wife, the authorities do not claim to have 'dissolved' the bond of the original marriage, as is the case with many of the civil codes of to-day. What we observe is, in fact, simply a 'dispensation' or 'licence' to take a second partner during the life-

[1] Prümmer, iii, p. 646.
[2] *S. Poen.*, 30 July, 1892; Prümmer, iii, p. 647.
[3] On a partial exception, *infra*, p. 72.
[4] Lacey, pp. 104, 127.

time of the first—a permission to engage in 'successive polygamy'.

These theological niceties do not concern us; nor does the consideration, also urged by Canon Lacey, that, since no valid marriage can be 'dissolved' by any human power, the word 'divorce' can never mean anything but mere separation.[1] The practical effect, which we all have in view when we speak of a couple being 'divorced', is that (unless the contrary is directly stated) each of them, in the eyes of the authority which pronounced their 'divorce', is free to marry another partner during the lifetime of the former one; and the word is so used in early and official documents, either absolutely, or with the addition of *a vinculo* or *quoad vinculum*.[2] It is in this sense that it will be used throughout the present book.

The significant feature about the word 'divorce', so understood, is that it implies first, that there has been a valid marriage between the two persons from the outset; and second, that some factor has intervened *since* the marriage, in virtue of which, by process of law, they are declared exempt from any

[1] Lacey, pp. x, 96. He consistently uses the word in this sense, and in this sense only—a fact which may on occasion deceive the unwary reader. It is so used also in canons 107, 108 of 1603; and, indeed, commonly until the nineteenth century.

[2] Unfortunately, however, it is also used, with or without the addition, for 'nullity' decrees. Hence in any document its meaning has to be scrutinized most carefully; and no certain inference can be drawn unless the author's usage in the particular case has first been ascertained—often a matter of great difficulty.

further matrimonial obligations to one another—even from the obligation of refraining from entering into a marriage contract with some other person during the first partner's lifetime. These two features make a clear line of demarcation between divorce and *nullity*, the third of the three words we have to consider.

In the case of *nullity*, what is alleged, or affirmed, is that there has never been a true marriage at all between the parties concerned, because one or more of the necessary minimum conditions was not present at the very outset. Either the parties (whether they knew it or not) stood to one another within the prohibited degrees of relationship; or the consent on one side was not full and free; or the necessary publicity and forms were not observed. Thus the contract was from the first an invalid one—besides being sinful in addition, if the parties knew that they were flouting, or leaving unfulfilled, one of the conditions regarded as essential by the society to which they belong.

In consequence, when the original and essential nullity of a marriage is established after due enquiry, it becomes the duty of the couple to separate, at all events until the marriage has been revalidated (if it is capable of revalidation) by one or other of the processes which we have yet to consider.[1] Similarly, from the moment that the nullity is established to the satisfaction of a responsible

[1] *Infra*, p. 81.

authority, each party is free to marry a new partner, for the simple reason that the previous ‘ marriage ’ was no marriage at all, and that this fact is now officially recognized by all concerned ; with the result that the new marriage will not violate the condition which in the Christian view is beyond question essential—that no previous partner shall be alive. Nothing could very well be sounder in principle. It is of course the case that, the laxer the divorce law of any community becomes, the less likely is the question of nullity to arise ; for if ‘ marriages ’ can be terminated at any moment by mutual consent, it is superfluous to enquire whether they are in fact real marriages or not. Nevertheless, it can be affirmed without hesitation that every society which has placed even the slightest restraint upon divorce recognizes that occasionally (at all events) the problem of nullity may arise, as a separate question, in cases where divorce cannot be granted.

II

By the fourth century of our era, as we have seen, the yoke of Christian marriage was proving too heavy for the half-converted masses who were beginning to invade the Church. It was not merely that men and women wished for release from partners whose infidelity, sinfulness, or uncongeniality exhausted their own capacity of endurance ; they wished, only too often, to be released from a first partner in order to unite themselves to a second. Hence mere separation, though always allowed to, and often enjoined upon, an innocent husband or wife whose partner had been guilty of marital infidelity, was not in itself enough. Reluctantly but inevitably, the Church was compelled to make concessions—to provide safety-valves—for the untamed sex-instincts of her children. By a curious fate, the two great branches of the Church took different courses. The Greeks found their safety-valve in divorce; the Latins theirs in nullity.

It is unnecessary to deal at any length with the history of divorce in the east; the facts are too well known.[1] As was only natural, the husband was the first to benefit by the concession. S. Basil, in A.D. 374, is already in the position that he dare not oppose the custom of contemporary Christianity, which allowed remarriage to a husband who had divorced his wife for adultery; [2] he even expresses himself doubtful as to whether discipline should be exercised against a guilty husband who remarries after being divorced for adultery. His contemporary, Epiphanius of Salamis, allows the innocent wife the same privileges as the innocent husband. So the process went on until, after the accession of Justinian at the beginning of the sixth century, the eastern system rapidly assumed the shape which it still has to-day.

[1] The authorities printed in full in Watkins, ch. vii.

[2] *Ep.* 188, can. 9.

By this system,

> "divorce and remarriage are allowed on various grounds, which no conceivable hypothesis could reconcile with the teaching of Christ. The Russian Church allows remarriage after divorce for adultery, and desertion, and banishment. The Greek Church allows it after divorce for treason, or the attempted murder of a wife by a husband, or a husband by a wife, or adultery, or circumstances suggesting adultery, or insanity,"

or the procuring of abortion.[1] It must, however, be noted that

> "the guilty parties in a divorce suit are under no circumstances permitted to marry one another. Even the death of the husband does not remove the bar . . . (Further) it is forbidden to the guilty wife to marry at all. An adulterer—that is to say a man who has sinned with a married woman—may marry a third person when he has fulfilled his term of canonical penance."[2]

It is universally agreed, even by their own canonists, that the eastern Churches have capitulated too far in this matter of divorce with remarriage. But recent schools of thought in the Church of England have gone far to exonerate them from blame, at all events as regards the remarriage of the so-called 'innocent partner'

[1] D. Stone, *Divorce and Remarriage* (Pusey House Occasional Papers, no. 7), pp. 17, 35, summarizing Watkins.

[2] Watkins, pp. 355, 356.

whose husband or wife has been divorced for infidelity. We will not anticipate here what will be said later as to the dialectical arguments by which the plea for divorce with remarriage is commonly upheld.[1] One argument, however, it will be convenient to consider at this point. It is often suggested that the practice in question can be vindicated by an appeal to one, if not two, sayings of our Lord recorded in S. Matthew's gospel. It is true that not even the text which offers most ground for this suggestion (Mt. 19 [9]) is quoted by any writer prior to the sixth century (even among those commentators who explicitly discuss it) as vindicating the practice. This, however, is not a final argument. The official Church and its theologians had not up to that period finally capitulated on the point; and those who pressed for the concession were not theologians, but worldlings, whose arguments would be based upon expediency and custom rather than on nice interpretations of points of Scripture. We are justified therefore, particularly in view of modern discussions, in giving somewhat detailed consideration to the question, Is there any reason to suppose that our Lord in any way sanctioned the remarriage of an innocent husband or wife, whose partner had been divorced for adultery, during the latter's lifetime?

[1] *Infra*, p. 95.

III

The author of the first gospel had at his disposal an embarrassing wealth of material on the subject of divorce. He knew of at least four different traditions or accounts of our Lord's sayings about it. Unfortunately, his use of this material makes it impossible for us to know (except in one case) [1] the exact form in which each of these accounts lay before him. But we may summarize them as follows, using the text of the Revised Version :—

(*a*) A brief saying (from the source commonly known as Q, embodied, with alterations from (*c*), in Mt. 5 ^{32}) of which the original form was probably (as in Lk. 16 ^{18}) : 'Everyone that putteth away his wife and marrieth another, committeth adultery : and he that marrieth one that is put away from a husband committeth adultery.'

(*b*) An extended account (Mk. 10 $^{2-12}$, embodied also, with alterations from (*d*), in Mt. 19 $^{3-9}$) of our Lord's answer to the question [2] : 'Is it lawful for a man to put away his wife ?' In the Marcan version, Jesus answers with another question, 'What did Moses command you ?' His hearers quote Deuteronomy 24 ^{1} (the permission of divorce),

[1] The Marcan account—(*b*) in the text above. Even here there may have been small divergences, but substantially Matthew knew it as it stands in Mk. 10 $^{2-12}$.

[2] Perhaps not a controversy with the Pharisees in Mk. ; the words 'there came unto Him Pharisees' do not occur in the western text. But the enquirers were obviously hostile ('tempting Him').

suggesting, however (curiously enough), that this is a *permission* ('suffered') and not a *command.* Jesus might very well have fastened upon this distinction between 'permission' and 'command' in order to develop His argument; in S. Matthew's version (Mt. 19 [8]) He is actually represented as doing so. But in S. Mark He goes straight to the heart of the matter. The divorce-regulation, whether permission or command, is merely a Mosaic ordinance introduced 'because of the hardness of men's hearts'. But the original divine command, from which it represents an unworthy declension, is to be found in Genesis 2 [24]: 'For this cause shall a man leave his father and mother, etc.'; which Jesus endorses with the emphatic words, 'What therefore God hath joined together let not man put asunder.' Finally, in a private conversation with the disciples He crystallizes the whole matter in words practically identical with the first half of saying (*a*), appending, however, a new second clause—'and if she herself shall put away her husband, and marry another, she committeth adultery'.[1]

(*c*) A brief and curious saying, known only

[1] Three further points of interest in the Marcan account: (1) Was it Mark himself who conflated the Q-saying ((*a*) above) with an account of teaching ending with the words 'put asunder'? The two seem to be originally dissociated, in so far as the Q-saying is addressed to the 'disciples in the house' and not to the original questioners; on the other hand, it is a favourite device of Mark (cp. 4 [10, 34], 7 [17], 9 [28], 10 [23]) to emphasize the

to the first evangelist (Mt. 5 [32] (conflated with (*a*)), and some important texts of 19 [9]) : ‘ Everyone that putteth away his wife maketh her an adulteress,’ —presumably because she must marry again to save herself from destitution, and such marriage (contrary to the permission of Deut. 24 [2]) is strictly forbidden in the new dispensation.[1] As the text stands in Mt. the words ‘ saving for the cause of fornication (*porneia*) ’ follow the words ‘ putteth away his wife ’. The purpose of this exceptive clause is difficult to see, since it in no way mitigates the clear teaching of the passage that even an innocent wife, if divorced, cannot remarry without being guilty of adultery. We may take our choice of several explanations :—

(i) The exceptive clause stood in the original

crucial words of a passage of teaching by introducing a pause, during which the disciples retire and are then addressed privately. (2) Did Mark receive the new second clause of the Q-saying from a primitive tradition, or did he introduce it himself? If the former, it probably represents a denunciation of Herodias analogous to John the Baptist's attack on Herod (so F. C. Burkitt, *Gospel History and its Transmission*, pp. 98–102) ; if the latter, it is an intelligent addition addressed by Mark to the Roman world (in which, in contrast to Jewish law, the woman was allowed to divorce her husband), to show that the prohibition of divorce affected both sexes equally. (3) Is it not possible that (*b*) was originally only a working up of (*a*), and consequently should not be reckoned as an independent tradition at all?

[1] Most texts of Matthew add : ‘ and whosoever shall marry her when she is put away committeth adultery.’ But Western authorities omit the words, and they are probably from (*a*), though the two may have been combined before they reached Matthew.

saying. If so, as we shall see,[1] the passage refers not to divorce at all, but to separation on grounds of nullity; though it is of course possible that Matthew took it to refer to divorce for adultery, overlooked the absurdity involved, and retained it for reason (ii) or (iii).

(ii) The clause is an unintelligent insertion, by Matthew himself or some early editor, designed to bring the passage into some kind of superficial agreement with Mt. 19 ⁹.

(iii) The clause was inserted (again either by Matthew or an editor), under the impression that *porneia* meant 'adultery',[2] as a highly scholastic recognition of the obvious truth, that if a woman is already an adulteress, divorce and remarriage do not, strictly speaking, 'make' her one.

(iv) There were rigorists in the early Church who *required* a husband to dismiss his wife if she committed adultery. Their opponents or critics might well have appealed to this text (in its original form) to prove that the Lord forbade the dismissal of a wife in any circumstances. The clause would then have been inserted by a rigorist scribe to suggest that the Lord's prohibition did not apply to the case of adultery—without necessarily suggesting that even in this case the husband would be free to remarry.

Whichever of these explanations we adopt, it is clear that the passage in no way sanctions the

[1] *Infra*, p. 64. [2] See *infra*, p. 62.

remarriage of the 'innocent' party after a divorce. It flatly prohibits the remarriage of a divorced woman, even if she be 'innocent' of any offence against her husband; and it says nothing at all as to the right of a man to remarry, for whatever reason he may have divorced his wife.

Two of S. Matthew's sources then, so far from sanctioning divorce with the right to remarriage where a partner has been guilty of adultery, prohibit the remarriage of divorced persons in any circumstances whatever, and assign this prohibition to the personal authority of our Lord. The third source, on the same authority, prohibits the remarriage of a divorced wife (even if 'innocent'), and gives no countenance to the remarriage of husbands. The fourth source, however, imports an element of uncertainty:—

(*d*) A controversy with the Pharisees, on the question: 'Is it lawful for a man to put away his wife *for every cause*?' (Mt. 19 [3]). In Mt. 19 [3-9] this controversy has been closely and not very skilfully [1]

[1] 'Not skilfully'—because while inserting a conclusion which appears to represent our Lord as admitting divorce in one case, Mt. retains the Marcan passage which represents Him as absolutely prohibiting it. Again, the words 'tempting Him', which he retains, are now meaningless. There is no longer any trap in the question, since a respectable body of Pharisees (the Shammaites) share the view which our Lord is represented as favouring. But there is a certain dexterity in the way in which Matthew rearranged the body of the Marcan material in order to emphasize the controversial character of the discussion; and particularly in his allotting the words "Moses *suffered* you" to Jesus, instead of to the questioners, as in the original tradition (cp. *supra*, p. 55).

knit up with the Marcan teaching-account (see (*b*) above)—so much so that we cannot say how much of it, apart from the opening question and the conclusion, belongs to the original separate tradition. Nor can we be certain what form the conclusion actually had in this (*d*) source, except that it was certainly not an affirmative answer to the original question. The answer as it stands in the text is, 'Whosoever shall put away his wife except for fornication, and shall marry another, committeth adultery.'[1] This has too many points in common with (*a*), (*b*), and (*c*) alike, for us to assume that it must necessarily be original[2]; and several possibilities remain open. The answer, in Matthew's source, may have been 'Not for every cause, but only for adultery' (i.e. the text as we have it). In that case tradition has represented our Lord as intervening in the well-known controversy between the great Pharisaic teachers Hillel (who allowed divorce on the slightest grounds) and Shammai (who allowed it only for adultery), and deciding on Shammai's side. But it may also have been a definite prohibition of divorce of any kind, as in (*a*) and (*b*). If this was the case, Matthew must have altered it because he was

[1] Some texts add 'And he that marrieth her when she is put away committeth adultery'; but this fits so badly to its context that it is almost certainly a scribal insertion from (*a*).

[2] There is, moreover, considerable uncertainty as to the text, which in some manuscripts is assimilated to (*c*), and in others to (*a*) (cp. previous note), in varying degrees.

personally interested in the Hillel–Shammai controversy, and wished to allege our Lord's authority for the stricter ruling.

The all-important point to recognize is that Matthew (whether following his source or not) intended the answer in 19 [9] to be an answer to the question in 19 [3], *and not necessarily to any other question.* He would not have enlarged the Marcan question by adding 'for every cause' (thus making it a direct reference to the Hillel–Shammai controversy) unless he intended to give an answer to this question in its new form; and this answer can be found nowhere except in the other vital alteration he has made in his Marcan material—the insertion of 'except for fornication'—which represents our Lord as assenting, *on this occasion*, to divorce with the possibility of remarriage. Thus the most that can be inferred from the passage is that a tradition was current which represented our Lord as saying, in effect, 'If I were to countenance divorce at all (though it must not be assumed that I do), I could never countenance it beyond the narrow limits laid down by Shammai.' He was, in fact, suggesting an interpretation, for Jews, of a passage in the Mosaic code, which so far as the new dispensation was concerned had been entirely abrogated.

It is obvious that such a tradition, which represents our Lord as intervening, by invitation, in a debate between two schools of Pharisaic casuists, and giving the weight of His authority to one of them, must be utterly apocryphal. If such a dispute had ever been brought to His notice at all, He would have dismissed it forthwith as one more example of Pharisaic hair-splitting. It is impossible, therefore, to use this passage as evidence that He ever countenanced the doctrine that remarriage is permissible after a partner has been divorced, even where the grounds of the divorce are that partner's adultery.

IV

There is not a single passage in the New Testament, therefore, which represents our Lord as giving any *general* permission for divorce with remarriage in the case of adultery, as distinct from the *special* reference to the Hillel–Shammai controversy contained in the apocryphal tradition (*d*); nor is there the slightest evidence that any such tradition was ever current. We cannot, of course, deny the abstract possibility that there *may* have been such a tradition; i.e., that the sentence, 'I say unto you, whosoever shall put away his wife except for fornication, and shall marry another, committeth adultery'[1] was current *without any*

[1] Even this does not explicitly sanction remarriage—for that we should need 'Whosoever shall put away his wife for fornication, and shall marry another, does *not* commit adultery'. But despite Lacey (p. 24), it would seem that the text sanctions remarriage *implicitly*, for (i) divorce without the right of remarriage was unknown in Judaism; (ii) Matthew could not have applied the text to the Pharisaic controversy unless he assumed it had

limiting context in certain circles as an utterance of Jesus. It is even possible that this tradition (if it ever existed) was the origin of tradition (*d*)—the latter story being fabricated to provide an interesting though fictitious setting for the logion. Such speculations, it cannot be said too emphatically, must remain for ever in the realm of mere hypothesis, as irresponsible as they are unverifiable. Yet even if the saying had been attributed to our Lord outside the context of the Hillel–Shammai controversy, it could not necessarily be inferred that its original intention was to represent Him as lending His authority to the practice of remarriage in the case of divorce for adultery.

The grounds on which this can be affirmed are philological. The customary New Testament word for a married woman's infidelity is *moicheia*. But the word used for the ground of divorce in both the Matthaean passages is not *moicheia*, but *porneia*. The meaning of *porneia* has been hotly disputed. It *may*, of course, be no more than a synonym for *moicheia*, but this cannot be taken for granted. Three other possibilities are suggested, the first of relatively slight importance, the other two of real significance :—

(i) 'Prolonged or promiscuous unchastity after

this meaning. It is no doubt true that no writer prior to the sixth century, even in the east, cites the passage as an authority for remarriage (Watkins, pp. 226, 364) ; but little can be deduced from this fact, since the idea of officially sanctioning remarriage does not appear until that period.

marriage.'[1] This does not help in the explanation of 5 [32]; and in 19 [9] merely alters the tradition to the extent of suggesting that our Lord, in His apocryphal excursion into Jewish casuistry, proposed a new solution of the problem—one even stricter than that of Shammai—neither prohibiting divorce altogether, nor yet allowing it to be assumed that his words were to be taken categorically, but restricting it (in the event of its being admitted at all) to cases in which the wife's offence was of a peculiarly odious kind.

(ii) 'prenuptial unchastity',[2] and

(iii) 'relationship within the prohibited degrees'.[3]

The importance of these last two suggestions, for each of which solid arguments have been adduced, is that they completely alter the character of the saying (19 [9]), which for the moment we are supposing to have existed as a separate logion without context. They make it not so much a statement about *divorce*, as a statement about *nullity* —for they suggest, as the ground for a valid separation with the right of remarriage, a factor which was present *before marriage*, and so if it invalidated the marriage at all, invalidated it from

[1] Cp. E. Evans, *Epistles to the Corinthians* (Clarendon Bible), p. 95.

[2] See the evidence in full, Watkins, pp. 168–70; and cp. E. G. Selwyn, *Theology*, xv (1927), pp. 89–101.

[3] W. K. Lowther Clarke, *Theology*, xv (1927), pp. 161–3; F. Gavin, *ib.*, xvi (1928), pp. 102–5.

the outset.[1] Whether the external evidence is sufficient to warrant the final adoption of either of these suggestions is uncertain; but one piece of internal evidence speaks strongly for the acceptance of one or other of them, as against the interpretation of *porneia* either as the equivalent of *moicheia*, or as meaning 'prolonged or promiscuous unchastity after marriage'. The argument is as follows:—

Whoever brought the saying into relation with the Hillel–Shammai controversy must have taken *porneia* in the sense of 'adultery after marriage' (for that was the point at issue among the Pharisees), and it matters little which of the two minor variations of this meaning he accepted. So far, we cannot say whether he interpreted our hypothetical tradition correctly or incorrectly; in any case he reduced it from a general assertion to a specific casuistical decision. But if *porneia* means adultery, the exceptive clause in 5 [32] has no real point; it is either an inept or an unwarranted addition (see (*c*) above). On the other hand, with either of the other meanings for *porneia*, the saying of 5 [32] becomes intelligible as it stands.[2] It now means, 'Whoever dismisses his wife, save for the cause of prenuptial unchastity' (*or*, on interpretation (iii), 'of relationship within the prohibited degrees') 'makes

[1] *Supra*, p. 49.

[2] Though not, of course, an original saying of our Lord's; see p. 66, n., below.

her an adulteress'. The implication is evident:—a wife may not be divorced, for in the almost inevitable event of her remarrying, that will make her an adulteress. But she *may* (and indeed *should*) be dismissed if her marriage is in fact null and void by reason of an antecedent impediment [1]; and thereafter—never having been truly married at all—she can take a new partner without fear of disobeying God's ordinance.

Thus the evidence of 5 [32] is in favour of the view that *porneia*, as used by one at least of Matthew's sources, means one or other of the 'diriment impediments' to marriage, to use the terminology of later canon law. If this is so, the original logion, whose existence (in the form as we now have it in Mt. 19 [9]) apart from any context we have been assuming, was probably no more than an assertion that remarriage after a decree of nullity is legitimate,[2] whereas remarriage after a divorce is not. This is a position with which the whole teaching of western Christianity, at all events, is in complete accord. It is true (as we have seen) that if the logion originally existed separately, and was brought into connection with the Pharisaic con-

[1] On 'impediments', *infra*, p. 76.

[2] It may be added that in this case, interpretation (iii) is much better than (ii)—for marriage within the Levitical degrees is a far more solid ground of nullity than prenuptial unchastity, and it is in the highest degree unlikely that the latter would have been mentioned, to the neglect of the former, as the *exclusive* ground on which a separation can be sanctioned.

troversy by the author of tradition (*d*), the latter must have misunderstood its purport. But that is nothing to the point. What emerges is a further argument of considerable weight against the view that there was ever any tradition associating the idea of the legitimacy of remarriage after divorce with the teaching of Jesus—except, of course, the ungainly fable of His intervention in the Hillel-Shammai controversy.

Incidentally, this conclusion confirms the view that the words of Mt. 19 [9] can never have existed as a separate saying outside the Hillel–Shammai context. If they ever did so, their reference, as we have just seen, was in all probability to the question of nullity, and not to that of divorce. But if it is unlikely that our Lord should have occupied Himself with the details of Pharisaic casuistry, it is incredible that He should have dealt with those of Christian canon law.[1] The hypothesis of an independent source (*e*) can therefore be finally rejected without the slightest hesitation.

The conclusion of this rather wearisome discussion can be very briefly stated. Before we could say that there was any evidence in the New Testament at all that our Lord authorized the remarriage of an 'innocent' party after a divorce, we should have to prove (i) that the saying of Mt. 19 [9] was at one time current as an independent logion without

[1] The same applies to 5 [32] if the exceptive clause stood in it originally, cp. *supra*, p. 64, n. 2.

context: and (ii) that its reference was to divorce on the ground of adultery, and not to nullity by reason of a diriment impediment. As to the second of these points, we have seen that in all probability the original reference of the saying (if it ever existed independently) was to nullity and not to divorce; as to the first, we have recognized that on the one hand there is no evidence whatever in its favour, whilst on the other hand there is very cogent evidence against it. There is, in fact, no case whatever for the suggestion that any New Testament source credited our Lord with sanctioning remarriage after divorce, even where the partner's adultery was the ground of the divorce; whilst three sources (or two at least, if (*b*) be taken as a working-up of (*a*)) unhesitatingly represent Him as forbidding it in every case.

V

We may notice here a further passage, known only to S. Matthew, which might have some bearing upon the question. To the incident of 19 $^{3-9}$ is appended an epilogue (19 $^{10-12}$), which runs as follows:—

"(10) The disciples say unto him, If the case of the man is so with his wife, it is not expedient to marry. (11) But he said unto them, All men cannot receive this saying, but they to whom it is given. (12) For there are eunuchs which were so born from their mother's womb; and there are eunuchs which were made eunuchs by men; and there are eunuchs which made themselves eunuchs for the kingdom of heaven's sake. He that is able to receive it, let him receive it."

Few passages in the synoptists present more problems than this. Its source or sources, its integrity, its original meaning, and the evangelist's purpose in placing it where it stands, are all open to question. For a detailed consideration of these points, the reader is referred to the appended note on page 157. Here we may notice simply that the evangelist *may* perhaps [1] have added it to mitigate the rigour of our Lord's teaching by suggesting that the prohibition of divorce and remarriage is merely a 'counsel of perfection' for a spiritual élite, and not a 'precept' for all men. It is indeed sometimes alleged that the words 'for the kingdom of heaven's sake' imply in addition that in our Lord's mind (at least as S. Matthew conceived it) the prohibition of divorce was not so severe as it might appear—for the kingdom was near at hand, and consequently the period of hardship would be only short; and that He wished to indicate this to the disciples. But this suggestion is impossible. The sense of verse 12 in this respect is unquestionable. Whoever those 'who have made themselves eunuchs' may be,[2] the intention of the words is to single them out for special praise, not to belittle their heroism. Their self-sacrifice is obviously regarded as undertaken to the glory and advance-

[1] See *infra*, p. 157. [2] *Infra*, p. 160.

ment of the 'kingdom', whether it come quickly or slowly; not as a merely spectacular display which is really much easier than it seems to be because the coming of the 'kingdom' will put an end to its rigours within a few months or years.

We will defer to a later chapter any general consideration of the possibility that our Lord's severer utterances can be discounted for modern purposes, either by the method of treating them as 'counsels of perfection' only, or by that of suggesting that He was deluded as to the nearness of the end, and consequently made upon His disciples demands for heroism which can safely be disregarded by those who are happily emancipated from this delusion.[1] Our immediate purpose is to consider whether these possibilities, in regard to the problem of divorce, receive any support from the present passage. That they do not do so is self-evident. The second of the two alternatives just mentioned is, as we have seen, wholly foreign to the sense of the epilogue. For the first alternative to be read into the passage, there would have to be some evidence at least that prior to Matthew's use of it, it stood in connection with a tradition of the divorce prohibition which could reasonably be regarded as genuine. No evidence of this kind is available—indeed the evidence is all the other way.

The epilogue, in the context in which Matthew

[1] *Infra*, pp. 99–103.

found or placed it, seems to concern only the Hillel–Shammai tradition, which we have seen to be unquestionably spurious—a fact which suggests the possibility that the epilogue is spurious too.[1] It is certainly no part of the Marcan tradition (Mk. 10 $^{2-12}$—see (*b*) above). Nor does it belong to tradition (*c*)—for if it had originally stood there, it would have been to the evangelist's interest to retain it. Can it originally have been connected with the Q-tradition (our (*a*), above)? At first sight this seems possible, and would indeed be likely if it could be shown that Mt. 19 ^{9} was in any way reminiscent of Q. But there is no such reminiscence. Mt. 19 ^{9} is based wholly and slavishly upon Mk. 10 $^{11, 12}$, and has nothing in common with Lk. 16 ^{18} (derived from Q) apart from what is also in Mk.; whereas Mt. 5 ^{32} agrees in a number of points with Lk. 16 ^{18} against Mk. 10 $^{11, 12}$, and Mt. 19 ^{9}. Thus it seems clear that in 19 ^{9} Matthew is using Mark, and Mark alone (apart from his own special insertions from source (*d*)); whilst in 5 ^{32} he is using Q and Q alone, with the addition of the exceptive clause. Since therefore *both* occasions of the Q-saying (Mt. 5 ^{32} and Lk. 16 ^{18}) lack the epilogue, we may say with confidence that it was unknown to Q.[2]

[1] Or, at all events, that its attachment to this tradition is no more than a piece of uninspired editing; *infra*, p. 158.

[2] Mk. 10 $^{11, 12}$ may also be a version of the Q-saying, as we have seen—this is further evidence that the epilogue is unknown

Thus none of the three extant traditions of our Lord's prohibition of divorce (excluding, of course, the spurious Hillel–Shammai story) knew of this epilogue. It may be added that the natural interpretation of the crucial words shows clearly that their original reference was not to divorce at all.[1] There is consequently no scriptural warrant whatever for suggesting that our Lord intended His prohibition to be taken merely as a 'counsel'. As for the view that He enacted it solely with regard to His personal and mistaken impression that the end of the world was imminent—if indeed such an impression can fairly be attributed to Him at all—this, as has already been indicated, is wholly alien to the sense of the passage.

to Q. It is true that Mt. 19 ^{9} (which is followed by the epilogue) is based upon Mk. 10 $^{11, 12}$, and so perhaps ultimately on Q. But since there is no *independent* reminiscence of Q in Mt. 19 ^{9}, it is clear that if he incorporated the epilogue here *it was not because he remembered it as belonging to the Q-version of the divorce-saying.*

[1] *Infra*, p. 160.

III

NULLITY

I

IT is not quite true to say that divorce, with the right of remarriage, has never been countenanced at all in the Latin Church. Theodore of Tarsus, the Greek archbishop of Canterbury of the end of the seventh century, was of course influenced by eastern policy and practice. His *Penitential* allows remarriage after divorce with considerable freedom—even to the extent that 'a husband convicted of crime, and sentenced to servitude, leaves his wife free to contract marriage with another man after the lapse of a year, provided that the former marriage was her first'.[1] Similar laxities are found in Irish canons; whilst the *Laws of Howel the Good*, in so far as they represent the practice of the Welsh Church in the tenth century, 'touch the lowest point ever reached by Christian legislation in the matter of marriage'.[2] On the Continent, a succession of councils under the Frankish domination produced canons allowing remarriage, not merely

[1] Watkins, p. 416.
[2] *ib.*, p. 423.

in the case of divorce for adultery, but also for other causes.[1]

More surprising still are a series of papal decisions which have caused Roman canonists some anxious moments. We know from Innocent III, for example,[2] that his predecessor Coelestine III attempted to extend the Pauline privilege to cases in which one partner in a Christian marriage 'had fallen into heresy or paganism'. Coelestine's statement was, in fact, so alarming and outspoken that Raymond of Pennafort, in compiling his appendix to Gratian's collection of canons, felt himself justified in omitting it.[3] Urban III (1185–7) had already attempted the same extension.[4] The most surprising case of all, however, is a decision of Gregory II, in his second letter to S. Boniface (A.D. 726),[5] which Roman apologists can only deal with by saying that it refers either to an antecedent impediment which as a fact had rendered the marriage null from the outset, or to a non-consummated marriage.[6]

For, as has already been noticed,[7] although a marriage is a true marriage from the moment that the contract has been assented to in due form, and

[1] Watkins, pp. 386–9. [2] c. 7, X. iv. 19.

[3] c. 1, X. iii. 33 (see Friedberg, *Corp. Jur. Can.* ii, p. 588, *pars decisa*); cp. *Conc. Trid.*, sess. xxiv, can. 5 de matr.

[4] c. 6, X. iv. 19. [5] Watkins, p. 377.

[6] e.g. Prümmer, iii, p. 470. No evidence is available to support either of these contentions.

[7] *Supra*, p. 20.

so before consummation has taken place, there has been a general tendency in western canon law to regard a non-consummated marriage as in some degree less indissoluble than a consummated one.[1] Thus a non-consummated marriage between Christians is held to be dissolved *ipso facto* by the solemn reception of one or other of the parties into a religious order,[2] and may be dissolved by papal dispensation for some other grave cause.[3] All modern Roman theologians further assert that, quite apart from the Pauline privilege, the Pope can dissolve a marriage contracted and consummated in heathendom; and most of them would add that he is able to do so even when it is consummated, or reconsummated, after the baptism of one partner.[4] Watkins has pointed out, with

[1] The English courts rarely grant a decree of nullity on grounds of lack of consent where consummation has taken place (cp. Halsbury, *Laws of England*, xvi, p. 279 for cases). This is not, however, an echo of the quasi-theological tendency noticed in the text, but simply a recognition of the fact that consummation is so convincing *primâ facie* evidence of consent that nothing short of overwhelming evidence to the contrary can invalidate it. See further, *infra*, pp. 84, 89.

[2] Innocent III, c. 14, X. iii. 32 (but see G. H. Joyce, *Christian Marriage*, pp. 430, 441, 450, 451); *Conc. Trid.*, sess. xxiv, can. 6.

[3] *Cod. Iur. Can.*, § 1119. The greatest of the Schoolmen, however, unanimously rejected this view; Joyce, *ubi sup.*, and p. 435.

[4] So Prümmer, iii, § 650 ('probabilius'—but I am informed that in a more recent edition (1925), which I have not seen, he regards it as certain); Capello ('*non solum probabilior sed certa*'). Cp. also E. J. Mahoney, 'Papal Dissolution of Marriage,' in *The Clergy Review*, vol. iv, no. 6 (Dec. 1932), pp. 503–6. The

regard to the first of these rulings (that concerned with *Christian* marriage) that it cannot logically be held with the doctrine that consummation is not of the essence of the marriage contract; [1] the same might be said of the remaining rulings too, if the view hitherto put forward (which Watkins unfortunately does not accept) of the indissolubility of marriage by natural law is accepted. But since no Anglican would regard the rulings in question as infallible, no argument can be based upon Watkins' contention. The rulings are to be noticed simply as further examples of the occasional admission of divorce in the west.

II

We need not spend time over this idiosyncrasy of western canon law. It was not to divorce that the west looked for its safety valve, but to nullity. The fact is a very surprising one. At first sight it seems impossible that the recognition that some

doctrine has been elaborated to account for certain actions and utterances of Pius V (*supra*, p. 25) and Gregory XIII (1585), in the matter of baptized heathen. Benedict XIV, however, was of the opinion that the actions, at least, were wholly explicable on the grounds of the Pauline privilege, and is at some pains to show (*De Syn. Dioc.*, xiii. 21. 4, 5) that the utterances did not mean what they appeared to mean. If the marriage is consummated or reconsummated after the baptism of *both* partners, no Pope could claim the power to dissolve it.

[1] Watkins, p. 134. His argument is simply that if the contract *de praesenti* is the sole essential, then a non-consummated marriage is as indissoluble as any other.

marriages are invalid by reason of conditions which were present *before* the parties contracted, should solve the difficulties of those who wish to be rid of their obligations because of circumstances which have arisen *after*—and perhaps long after—the marriage took place. But there can be no two opinions as to the facts ; and although the question of nullity does not occupy an extensive place in modern legal practice, its history is of sufficient interest to call for a brief consideration.

The idea of nullity is bound up with a technical term which is of vital importance both for the history and for the theory of marriage—the term *impediment*. Where two persons are so circumstanced that in any 'marriage' contracted between them one of the necessary minimum conditions to which we have already alluded is or would be absent, there is said to be an *impediment* to their marriage. Thus, if for any reason they have not given the necessary public notice of their intention, or contract without the necessary number of witnesses (whatever the State or Church to which they belong may actually consider necessary in the matter), the impediment of *clandestinity* stands in the way of their marriage. If, again, they stand within the degrees of prohibited blood-relationship to one another (however those degrees may be defined by the community to which they belong), they suffer from the impediment of *consanguinity*, and so forth.

There are a certain number of impediments

which occur in almost every civilized code. But the scientific or logical classification even of these undisputed impediments is a matter of extreme difficulty, and many ingenious schemes have been devised. The simplest, perhaps, is that which distinguishes them according to the effect they have upon any 'marriage' contracted in their despite. We are not considering here whether the parties, to whose marriage such an impediment exists, will be punished or not if nevertheless they attempt to contract. On that point it is enough to say that if the marriage were made in good faith, or in ignorance of the impediment, punishment would be extremely unlikely; if it represented a deliberate defiance of a known impediment, and still more if the defiance involved wilful suppression or perjury, punishment would be justly deserved. Quite apart from this, however, is the effect which an impediment, whether known or unknown, may legally have upon the validity of the 'marriage' of those who are subject to it.

From this point of view an impediment may be regarded as belonging to one of three classes—non-prohibitive, irremovable, and removable. The first class is technically known as *impedient* ('obstructive'), the second and third are both *diriment* ('destructive'). But the difference between the two last is so great that it is better to treat them as wholly separate classes.

Non-prohibitive impediments can be easily dismissed from consideration; for although they may render those who contract in defiance of them liable to discipline or punishment, they cannot invalidate the marriage. In canon law, for example, Christians are forbidden to marry in Lent. But if they do so, while both they and the priest who celebrates the wedding are liable to ecclesiastical censure, the Church does not consider itself entitled to declare the marriage void. It was irregular in one particular, but it is certainly final and valid in essence; and no power on earth can declare it to be invalid. It may be noticed that English statute law does not recognize any non-prohibitive impediments.

Irremovable impediments are impediments as to which, if they are brought to his notice, the appropriate judicial authority (whoever he may be) has no option but to declare the marriage null and void from the outset.[1] Such impediments, in all civilized communities, are those created by close blood-

[1] In English law (cp. Lord Hardwicke's Act of 1753 and Lord Lyndhurst's Act of 1835) marriages contracted with irremovable impediments are not merely 'voidable', but actually 'void to all intents and purposes whatsoever'. The effective difference would appear to be that under the old canon law, though such a 'marriage', once the impediment had been made public, must be declared void, this declaration could only take place during the lifetime of both parties. Failing this, the marriage was treated in effect as valid as regards the rights of the offspring, etc. Under English law, on the other hand, such marriages must be declared invalid, even if the impediment is only discovered after the death of one or both of the parties; hence the impediment jeopardizes the rights of all descendants of the union to an indefinite extent. See Halsbury, xvi, p. 283.

relationships—the relationship of father and daughter, brother and sister, and so forth. As a category, they present no more difficulty than the non-prohibitive impediments. They are of such gravity that the community refuses in any case (however extenuating the circumstances may be) to recognize a marriage contracted in their despite. In English civil law the only irremovable impediments are the prohibited degrees of consanguinity and affinity (Archbishop Parker's Table, less certain relationships which have been removed from the list in recent years [1]); prior marriage not dissolved by decree absolute; and the insanity of either party at the actual time of marriage.

The greatest difficulties in the history of marriage have been created by the class of impediment which we have called *removable*, especially where the impediment has been discovered or declared after the ceremony has taken place. If the impediment is declared beforehand, the remedy is simple: the appropriate authority may, in its discretion, and at the request of both parties, remove it. In ecclesiastical law this process is known as *dispensation*. Thus in the matter of clandestinity, for example, the bishop's or archbishop's licence is a dispensation granted to the two persons concerned, which exempts them from the necessity of the publication of banns. In the middle ages vast

[1] E.g. deceased wife's sister (1907); deceased brother's widow (1921); uncle and niece, etc. (1931).

numbers of impediments were removed by dispensation—at a price. Marriage with a deceased wife's sister, for example, could be (and under modern Roman canon law can still be) celebrated if a dispensation had been secured; for England it became an irremovable impediment by the legislation of Henry VIII, and remained so (with some uncertainty till the time of Chief Justice Vaughan) [1] up to 1907, when, so far as the civil law was concerned, it ceased to be an impediment altogether. It must not be assumed, however, that dispensations were always given as a matter of course; the canon law prescribed that even though an impediment were removable, it could only be dispensed if some grave cause for such a procedure were adduced.[2]

Dispensation is not known in modern English statute law, except in so far as marriage by ecclesiastical licence (in lieu of banns) is recognized and upheld by the civil power, and marriage by a registrar's certificate with licence, in lieu of notice, was instituted by the Act of 1836. The reason for this disappearance of dispensation from English law is obvious. Henry VIII's legislation introduced the principle that (apart from formalities) no impediments should be allowed save those

[1] Lacey, p. 184; with references there.

[2] On the 16 grave causes admitted in modern Roman canon law (*Propaganda*, May 9, 1877), see e.g. Tanquerey, *Synopsis Theol. Mor.*, i, pp. 669 ff.

enacted by 'God's law'; and from such impediments, obviously enough, no human power can dispense. Nevertheless, 'dispensation' from the impediment of prior marriage was in effect given to individuals on occasion by special Act of Parliament, up to the passing of the Divorce Act of 1857; and it has to be admitted that the English Church seems to have acquiesced in this practice, though perhaps under duress.[1]

It is when a removable impediment is only declared or discovered *after* the marriage of the parties, that the situation becomes most complicated. Unless some step is taken to remedy the defect, any judicial authority to whose notice the circumstances are brought will have no option but to declare the marriage null and void. But the defect can be remedied, and this in different ways, according to the nature of the impediment and the actual circumstances of the particular case. *One* condition however must be satisfied before any rectification is possible:—*both parties must be agreed that the 'marriage', which has hitherto been invalid, shall continue as a true marriage.*[2] In default of such agreement, no court (whether secular or religious) which takes cognizance of the case will have any other alternative (assuming the existence of the

[1] Lacey, p. 202, with refs.; and on the hesitations of Anglican divines, and certain cases in which ecclesiastical courts are alleged to have given similar dispensations, see Dibdin and Chadwyck-Healey, *English Church Law and Divorce*, *pass.*

[2] On this 'renewal of consent', see *infra*, pp. 83–4.

alleged impediment to be proved) than to declare the marriage null.[1]

In canon law, some of these removable impediments discovered after marriage can be dealt with by ecclesiastical authority alone—such impediments, for example, as clandestinity, and the 'removable' degrees of consanguinity and affinity. Here, of course, if there is doubt as to the existence of the 'impediment', the appropriate court must first investigate it. Thus in the case of Henry VIII's suit for nullity against Catherine, the point at issue was whether an impediment which had been formally dispensed with before marriage could be treated as an impediment still in vigour after marriage—a difficult legal problem, though precedent was on Henry's side. In a well-known case about to be discussed, the alleged coercion of the bride had similarly to be made the main subject of enquiry. But if the existence of the impediment has been proved, the court may in its discretion, and at the request of both of the parties, issue a *post factum* dispensation, on the same principles as those which govern pre-nuptial dispensations. No such *post factum* dispensations are known in modern English law; but they played a large part in mediaeval canon law, and still do so in the modern Roman code.

[1] For cases of defective consent in which decrees of nullity have been granted by English secular courts, *supra*, p. 74, n. 1. A very recent case occurs in the *Times Law Reports*, vol. xlix, no. 6 (Dec. 16, 1932)—Kelly, otherwise Hyams *v.* Kelly.

The *post factum* dispensation, however, has the disadvantage that it only validates the marriage from the moment when it is granted; whereas what is required by the parties is as a rule a retrospective validation from the moment at which the marriage was solemnized. In the canon law, this is achieved by a process known as *sanatio in radice*; under English law nothing short of an Act of Parliament can effect it. From time to time, for example, marriages are by accident contracted without the full legal formalities, e.g. in a building not registered for the purpose, or before an agent without proper jurisdiction. In such cases Parliament has shown itself not unwilling to make good the defect by retrospective legislation, if the persons concerned ask for it.[1]

Many removable impediments, however, can be dealt with by the mere process of nature, or by the action of both the parties, or even one of the parties concerned alone. Thus in English law, in the case of a marriage contracted between two persons either of whom is below the age of consent, 'if they agree to continue together at the age of consent, no new marriage is necessary'.[2] And in

[1] For the relevant Acts of Parliament, Halsbury, *Laws of England*, xvi, pp. 308, 309.

[2] *E. Br.*[11], xvii, p. 756, n. 3; cp. Halsbury, xvi, p. 282. In Latin canon law, the same principle is observed, but the parties must 'renew consent' before a priest and witnesses. Similarly of 'inability to consummate', which renders a marriage only voidable, and not void, in English law. Halsbury, xvi, pp. 283, 470–2.

general any kind of defective consent (as, for example, that resulting from coercion) can be regularized by a simple renewal of consent between the parties—such renewal being reasonably deduced from their voluntarily continuing to dwell together as husband and wife.[1] Further, if the defective consent was on one side only (as in the cases, popular with dramatists, in which the lady who is married is not the lady whom the bridegroom intended to marry), nothing more is needed to validate the marriage than that the partner who was not truly consenting at the time of the union should accept it willingly as a *fait accompli*—the other partner, perhaps, being equally ignorant both of his original unwillingness to acquiesce in the union, and of his subsequent change of mind.

III

It is no part of the purpose of this book to attempt to draw up a list of impediments such as would satisfy the ideals of natural justice ; nor yet

[1] 'Since an express renewal of consent is not demanded by natural law'—Prümmer, iii, p. 634. In English law, the fact of consummation is normally regarded as final evidence of consent (*supra*, p. 74). But by canon law there must be a 'new act of will' for such renewal of consent (*Cod. Jur. Can.*, § 1834)—consequently a mere despairing or ignorant acquiescence would not suffice ; though how such a 'new act of will' can either be proved or disproved, except by cohabitation, it is hard to discern. For the bearing of this on a recent case, *infra*, p. 89. In the Roman canon law many clandestine marriages can be validated by a due renewal of consent between the parties before the parish priest and two witnesses ; others require a dispensation.

to discuss such aspects of the question as are still matters of live interest in the English courts. To the ordinary reader the whole question of impediments must appear highly academic. Indeed, English law (as we have seen) has wisely reduced the number of irremovable impediments to such circumstances, including the forbidden degrees, as are 'prohibited by God's law'; and recognizes no category of removable impediments which may be remedied by process of law, except in the rare case where some necessary legal formality has unintentionally been overlooked, but may be rectified by a private Act of Parliament. The consequence is that nullity suits are relatively uncommon in England.

In this situation the Church of England has with equal wisdom concurred. But if we consider the history of western Christendom as a whole, it is easy to see that the whole system of impediments, especially in its infinite mediaeval ramifications, together with the possibility of nullifying unsatisfactory marriages which it opened up, offered a loophole as effective in its own way as the practice of divorce *a vinculo* adopted by the Greeks. In the small and highly localized communities of the middle ages, any couple were almost certainly related to one another within the prohibited degrees of the elaborate and extended tables of consanguinity and affinity then in vogue; and where a majority of marriages suffered from some degree of informality, clandestinity could easily be alleged. Thus a man or woman who wished to be rid of his or her partner on some ground which in actual fact in no way invalidated the marriage, would not find it difficult to discover a plea specious enough to suggest that the marriage was invalid from the outset; and so to secure the desired end by a means never intended for that purpose.

In this respect, no historian has ever thought it necessary to question the accuracy of the statement contained in Henry VIII's revolutionary Act of the year 1541. The mediaeval system, the preamble says, was one

> 'whereby not only much discord between lawful married persons hath (contrary to God's ordinance) arisen, much debate and suit at the law, with wrongful vexation and great damage of the innocent party, hath been procured, and many just marriages brought in doubt and danger of undoing, and also many times undone, and lawful heirs disinherited,' . . .

but also

> 'marriages have been brought into such an uncertainty thereby, that no marriage could be surely knit and bounden, but it should lie in either of the parties' power and arbiter, casting away the fear of God, by means and compasses . . . to defeat the same.'[1]

The Latin Church of to-day is, in its own way, a reformed Church as much as any other. There

[1] 32 Henry VIII, c. 38.

can be no doubt that the abuses of the nullity decrees of the middle ages have been in the main removed. But an uneasy suspicion lingers in many minds that nullity suits are still sometimes used as convenient substitutes for that divorce which western canon law so stringently forbids. Every such case must be tried before two separate courts, and the nullity affirmed in each. But the first court is merely diocesan, and the second court may be no higher than that of a metropolitan.[1] There are more than 250 provinces, and 900 dioceses, in the Roman world; hence it is possible that the administration of the law differs widely in different countries. In the ecclesiastical court of Quebec, for example, as recently as 1910, a husband married *in facie ecclesiae* in 1904, and who had lived with his wife for some time, was accorded a decree of nullity on the ground that the two parties, unknown to both of them at the time of their marriage, were the descendants of the same great-great-grandparents married in 1781, and had contracted without a dispensation.[2]

In about 50 cases a year, however,[3] the second court which retries the case is the Roman Rota, and here it is more possible to judge of the extent to which the decree of nullity, when given, would

[1] F. J. Sheed, *Nullity of Marriage*, p. 57.

[2] Despatie *v.* Tremblay, *Law Reports* (1921), 1, A.C., p. 700; cited by G. R. Y. Radcliffe, in *The Bell Yard*, May, 1932.

[3] Sheed, pp. 71, 72.

satisfy the demands of natural justice. One such case, which achieved notoriety because of the social standing of the persons concerned, was decided in 1926.[1] The couple were married in 1895, in America, neither of them being at that time of the Roman obedience. Ten years later they ceased to live together, two children having been born to them. In 1920 they obtained a civil divorce, and each remarried. In 1926, the lady, who had by this time become a Roman Catholic, brought the suit for nullity, which was granted first at Southwark, and then, on retrial, at Rome.

The grounds of the petition were that the bride had been forced into the marriage unwillingly through fear of her mother, who exercised 'every sort of constraint, pushed even to physical violence'; coupled with the insistent suggestion that 'if the petitioner opposed her will, it was, seeing her state of health, a vexation such that it might lead to her death'. The evidence of the constraint exercised, of the daughter's resistance, and of her repugnance to her husband, was in itself very strong. But it was open to the obvious objection that the wife had undoubtedly acquiesced in the marriage for ten years, and so might reasonably be considered to have 'renewed her consent'. To this it was replied that she was probably unaware that want of consent was a ground of nullity, and

[1] For the facts, with a translation of the findings of the court, see Sheed, pp. 63–70.

so supposed that she had no other alternative than to acquiesce.[1] Such a plea, it may be hazarded, would scarcely have met with acceptance in our English court, where the fact of the ten years' cohabitation would have been taken as final evidence of consent.[2] For even if the maxim, *Ignoratio juris nulla excusatio*, may sometimes be legitimately set aside, in the present instance it seems to have been flouted with a recklessness which no impartial mind could applaud.

These, however, are questions for the lawyers to decide. To the lay mind what was disquieting, and still remains disquieting, about the case, was the nature of the evidence on which the decree was granted. It appears to have been entirely, or almost entirely, evidence of persons who were interested in obtaining the decree—the petitioner herself, whose second marriage, unless the decree were obtained, was invalid and unlawful in the eyes of the Church which she had joined; her aunt, her mother, and her mother's friend. Again, the events to which the evidence referred were thirty years old; which meant that, quite apart from the possibility that the witnesses' perspectives may themselves have altered, it would be extremely difficult for the *defensor vinculi*[3] to obtain the purely objective evidence of detached observers, to say nothing of rebutting evidence.

[1] Sheed, p. 69. [2] Cp. *supra*, pp. 74, n. 1; 84.

[3] The official corresponding in canon law to the King's Proctor.

Finally, the official report of the case makes it clear, not merely that hearsay evidence was admitted (—' This was also the opinion of the doctor, which was known to me from a friend of my mother, Mrs. Jay, who learnt it from her '—) but that it was considered to be of sufficient importance to be mentioned in the findings of the court.[1] To the ordinary mind, therefore, it must still remain an open question whether the laws of evidence governing procedure in the Roman courts do not tell unduly against presumptive marriages; with the result that the safety-valve of which the middle ages availed themselves so freely cannot be said to be entirely ineffective even to-day.

[1] It is only fair to add that the report is ambiguous here. The statement about the doctor may have been adduced as evidence that the mother's health was in fact precarious. On the other hand, it may have been regarded merely as evidence that the petitioner had been led to suppose that the doctor held this view. In the first case, its inadmissibility is certain; in the second its admissibility is doubtful. If the second construction is to be put upon it, it is curious that it appears in the findings as a statement by the petitioner as to what Mrs. Jay had said, and not as a statement by Mrs. Jay (who was actually a witness in the case) that she had said such-and-such things.

Cancelled from
Gladstone's Library
08 MAR 2023

IV

INDISSOLUBILITY

I

THERE is, as we have seen, no New Testament basis whatever for the suggestion that our Lord sanctioned remarriage during the lifetime of the first partner in the case of an 'innocent' person who has secured a divorce. The nearest approach to this is a tradition, generally agreed to be unauthentic, that on one occasion, when asked to arbitrate between two casuistical interpretations of the Jewish law of divorce, He expressed a preference for the stricter one. On the other hand, our review of the synoptic evidence shows that there is an extraordinarily strong New Testament tradition that He emphatically condemned remarriage after divorce in all cases. This tradition appears not only in the synoptists, but also in S. Paul, who writes to the Corinthians in or about the year A.D. 55:—'Unto the married I give charge, *yea not I, but the Lord*, that the wife depart not from her husband (but and if she depart, *let her remain unmarried*, or else be reconciled to her husband): and that the husband leave not his wife.'[1] Later in the chapter he reverts to the same instruction: 'A wife is bound for so long time as her husband liveth: but if the husband be dead she is free to be married to whom she will, only in the Lord.'[2] In the Epistle to the Romans (A.D. 56) the same aphorism is used, with only verbal alterations, to illustrate a theological point; but it closes with the significant sentence, 'So then if, while the husband liveth, she be joined to another man, she shall be called an adulteress: but if the husband die, she is free from the law, so that she is no adulteress, though she be joined to another man.'[3]

[1] 1 Cor. 7 [10, 11].

[2] 1 Cor. 7 [39]. Inferior MSS. add 'by law' after the word 'bound'; but this is unquestionably an interpolation from Rom. 7 [2] (see next note).

[3] Rom. 7 [2, 3]. A difficulty is created here by the fact that S. Paul says that the indissoluble tie which binds the wife to the husband till death is 'by law', and the fact that he is speaking 'to men that know the law' implies that he means the Jewish law, not the Christian one. But while the Jewish law prohibited a wife from divorcing her husband, she was perfectly free if divorced, or if by public process or mutual consent she induced her husband to divorce her (see Abrahams, *Studies in Pharisaism and the Gospels*, pp. 70, 75, etc.), to marry again (Deut. 24 [2]). Thus either S. Paul is speaking inaccurately, and meant to say: 'No woman has a right to leave her husband; she is his by law *as long as he chooses to claim her*, and in all ordinary cases this means until his death'—a premise which would have completely satisfied the requirements of his analogy: or (*b*) he is referring to the new Christian tradition, which refused remarriage to the woman even if she were repudiated unjustly. In this case the reference to the 'law' is either to the 'Christian law', or (more probably) a careless introduction of a phrase from the main theme of the passage

It is noteworthy that S. Paul says nothing as to the remarriage of the man. But since he forbids either the husband or the wife to seek a divorce, or to act as though one had been obtained, it is natural to suppose that he would insist on the principle of ' remaining unmarried ' as much in the one case as in the other. Even if this instruction, however, refers to the woman alone, it represents an epoch-making advance upon contemporary practice. Both Jewish and Roman custom allowed a wife, who (by whatever legal means and for whatever cause) was divorced from her husband, complete liberty of remarriage. S. Paul introduces his startling innovation without the slightest apparent recognition of its revolutionary character. He quotes it as a word of the Lord which will be accepted as such without challenge. Both these facts go far to prove that long before the synoptic tradition had been reduced to its present form, and within twenty-five years of the Crucifixion itself, there was absolute unanimity in the Church that our Lord had proclaimed the indissolubility of marriage.

These facts are of the greatest importance. Apostolic Christianity set itself to revolutionize the temper of existing society. It proclaimed new

(the Christian's freedom from law). But it cannot be denied that interpretation (*a*) is the more likely, and therefore the Romans passage is very doubtful evidence for the tradition, though it does not in any way tell against it.

virtues and personal duties of the most penetrating kind. But in no other matter than this of marriage did it show any inclination to alter the *institutions* of contemporary society. It accepted slavery, social inequality, the existing wage-system, the Roman imperial rule and taxation, the legal obligations of the empire's subjects. Lax as contemporary marriage customs were, they were by no means the only, and probably not even the worst, of the social evils of the day. Why, then, should the Church have selected this one point as the place in which to raise the standard of revolt? The answer is almost inevitable. The apostles took no action in the matter of slavery (for example), because they had no word of the Lord about it. But they set themselves to purify the existing marriage system because they had an unalterable conviction that it was their Master's will. And it is difficult to see any source from which they could have obtained that conviction except from Jesus Himself, of whose emphatic statements the true record is preserved in the synoptists.

Anyone, therefore, who in the face of the internal evidence of the gospels professes to believe that Jesus never condemned remarriage after divorce, must reckon with the external evidence as well. He will have to show reason why the Church fabricated sayings of our Lord to this effect, and did not fabricate similar sayings condemning in the same explicit fashion slavery, and imperialism, and other abuses of the day—particularly we may say, slavery, which the modern Christian conscience condemns with far greater unanimity than it does divorce. Nor will he be able to discover any reason whatever for this amazing phenomenon, for no contemporary sect or school of philosophy is known which could have influenced the early Church in this direction. There are those who profess to find it almost incredible that our Lord should have spoken so explicitly on the subject of marriage. The answer to this is simple: the attitude of the early Church in the matter makes it even more incredible that He should *not* have done so.

II

This, however, does not dispose of the question. It has become a common practice nowadays to insist that our Lord's words about divorce cannot be taken at their face value. That He uttered them is admitted; that He intended them to be understood literally is denied. This is commonly expressed by the vague phrase: 'He was stating an ideal, but was not legislating.' The phrase in itself can be dismissed without further consideration. Our Lord never 'legislated', in the strict sense of the word: that is to say, He never ordained temporal penalties for those who disregarded or disobeyed His maxims. In this respect the teaching on divorce is in exactly the same position as any other part of our Lord's ethical teaching ; and anything that applies to it applies equally to every part of His message.

It is to be supposed that those who use this phrase really intend it to cover some other idea which they have failed to make clear even to themselves. And as a fact we can discern no less than four different lines of argument emerging here and there in support of the general theory that the words are not to be taken at their face value. Any or all of these may be intended when we are told that ' Jesus was not legislating '. It is well to take them separately, if only to notice how an ambiguous and question-begging phrase can gain wide currency on the slenderest of real grounds.

First of all, we are often told that our Lord's words about divorce and remarriage are not plain matter-of-fact statement, but a piece of picturesque oriental exaggeration, designed to drive home a moral lesson with peculiar force. The parallels that are quoted include the commands to turn the other cheek, to ' go with him twain ', to ' take no thought for the morrow ' ; the prohibition of saying ' Thou fool ' to a brother ; whilst analogous metaphors are to be found in the sayings about the camel and the needle's eye, about cutting off hand and foot, about faith moving mountains, and others which will easily recur to memory. Similarly, it is suggested, the prohibition of divorce and remarriage is an exaggeration which need not and indeed should not be taken literally. It cloaks no more than a general injunction to live the sex-life with reasonable moderation.

The difficulty about this interpretation must be obvious to everyone. It is simply that whereas the other instances quoted are genuinely ' picturesque ', this one is merely prosaic. The uprooted mountains, the lilies of the field, the eager wayfarer pressed into imperial service,[1] the turned cheek, the camel and the needle—this is the stuff of which poetry is made. And when our Lord needed a picturesque phrase to express the idea of moderation in sex, He could use one which, macabre though it is, nevertheless makes a vivid appeal to the imagination.[2] A man must be wholly void of literary sense to suggest that the divorce teaching comes into anything like the same category as these others. If *they* are compact of imagination, *its* fibre is wholly trite and matter of fact.

Alternatively, it is alleged that the divorce-sayings are not ' unchanging principles ', but ' variable rules '. This distinction between ' principles ' and ' rules ' is a favourite one nowadays, and is applied in almost every field in which, wisely or unwisely, it is desired to tread out a new path. But on examination it cannot be found to apply to the present case. A ' rule ' is the application of a ' principle ' to a particular set of circumstances, and

[1] The meaning of ' compel thee ' in Mt. 5 [41].
[2] Mt. 19 [12]—assuming the words to be genuine.

so long as the circumstances do not alter in any essential respect, the 'rule' remains as invariable as the 'principle' to which it gives expression. There are, indeed, many differences of circumstance between the modern world and the Palestine of our Lord's own day. But can it with reason be asserted that any one of them affects the state of marriage in any material particular? Every one of the reasons urged to-day in favour of divorce with the right to remarry was known to the Jews [1]; and it is ridiculous to suggest that they operate more intensely now than they did then. The problems of sex are not very greatly affected by changes in social or economic systems, nor by the progress of education and civilization. For sex is a more fundamental principle than any of these others, and so remains unaltered through all their changes.

It follows, therefore, that our Lord's teaching upon sex has the same value, authority, and application to-day as it has ever had. We may call the divorce sayings a 'rule' if we will, but if so they are an invariable rule, expressing an invariable principle, because no change of circumstances except a universal and revolutionary modification of the sex-instinct can affect their relevance to life.[2]

A third view suggests that the divorce-sayings

[1] See I. Abrahams, *op. cit.*, pp. 75 ff.

[2] It might be replied that the abandonment of the apocalyptic world-outlook was such a 'change of circumstance'. This view is dealt with below, pp. 101–3.

of the Gospels are not 'precepts' but 'counsels'. The distinction between counsels and precepts is a well-known one. A 'counsel' is a maximum standard (or ideal), at which men ought to aim; a 'precept' is a minimum standard, below which they must not fall. Of the practical value of this double standard in morality I have written elsewhere [1]; as also of its dangers.[2] All that need be said here is this. Unless the distinction is to lead to moral degradation and chaos, the precept must be clearly understood to be a mere precept, or minimum, and not a norm; and the corresponding counsel must be kept before all men's eyes as something at which all ought to aim, and not simply a special category of virtue reserved for a saintly élite.

The practical result is as follows. When it comes to actual statement, the counsel may be left relatively vague, for the possibilities of moral progress are infinite. But at all costs the precept must be stated in the most definite terms, and all must understand that it is a minimum which can only be neglected or disregarded at the risk of moral and spiritual disaster. For if the minimum is not clearly stated, and yet it is recognized that there *is* a minimum, and that if it is respected the worst penalties can be avoided, there will result an inevitable tendency to express this minimum in ever lower and lower terms. The process will be that

[1] *The Vision of God*, pp. 240–53. [2] *ib.*, pp. 246, 257, 520.

of which everyone is painfully conscious in the matter of Lenten resolutions. Our Lenten resolutions are embraced not as the maximum at which we aim during Lent; but rather as an attempt to set ourselves a slightly higher minimum standard than usual. But if we leave the tiniest loophole in a resolution, we know only too well how we tend to take advantage of it, until by the end of Lent our minimum standard has become a very tattered, inadequate affair. And this has always been the case on the wider stage of Church history. Even where 'precepts' have been very clearly enunciated, it has been difficult to maintain them at a creditable level; but if there has been the slightest ambiguity in them, society—even Christian society—has invariably interpreted them in the lower rather than in the higher sense.

There are suggestions in the gospels—or, rather, in the gospel of S. Matthew—that our Lord employed the method of counsel and precept in His teaching.[1] Indeed, as we have seen,[2] the first evangelist may have believed that our Lord's divorce-teaching was of the nature of a 'counsel' only. It seems unlikely that these suggestions are true to fact; they probably emanate from the ecclesiastical mind of the author of the first gospel, or from the practical pastoral experience of some part of the primitive Church. But if our Lord did employ this method, it is incredible that He should have

[1] *The Vision of God*, p. 69. [2] *Supra*, p. 68.

neglected what may be called its first rule, and omitted not merely to define the precept—the minimum standard—clearly, but even to state it at all. Yet this is the case if the proposed solution of our problem be adopted. The ' counsel '—the maximum—is very definite: ' No divorce in any case.' But what is the precept, the minimum? We are left entirely in the dark on the point; and can only assume that those who put this interpretation upon our Lord's teaching would have us believe that, as far as the minimum—the precept—was concerned, He was prepared to admit a laxity as great as that of society around. For that clearly was the result to which His teaching would have tended, if the divorce prohibitions were ' counsels of perfection ' only, which did not bind everyone, whilst nothing was said about any obligation by which everyone *was* to consider himself bound.

A fourth suggestion, which might be covered by the nebulous phrase ' not legislation, but ideals ', is bound up with an entire theory as to our Lord's self-consciousness which cannot well be considered here. Briefly, it is the doctrine that Jesus mistakenly thought of Himself as the Messiah who was to bring the world-era to an end within a very few years, and usher in a supernatural kingdom of God which should be a reign of perfect bliss for all who inherited it. But to make sure of their heritage, His disciples must for the brief intervening period lead a life of special asceticism and self-denial, and for this purpose (it is suggested) He elaborated a code of ethics which heroic resolution might enable individuals to obey for a few years, though no society could adopt it as a permanent and enduring system.

From such a theory an obvious inference can be drawn. If any part of our Lord's ethical teaching is felt to be oppressively severe, it can be referred to the 'interims-ethik' which emanated from this eschatological hallucination. We may revere it as an ideal, but we are not required to act upon it as a law. In particular, we may deal with the teaching about divorce after this fashion.[1]

This 'apocalyptic' theory of our Lord's purposes has waned in popularity now that the first flush of enthusiasm which greeted its appearance has died down. Confining ourselves to its ethical side alone, we notice simply as an insuperable difficulty that the most ascetic of our Lord's sayings are nowhere found in connection with His eschatological discourses; whilst the same eschatological outlook in contemporary Judaism is wholly free from ascetic interests. It is true that in a passage in which he commends virginity *on other grounds* (1 Cor. 7 [25-38]), S. Paul asserts that 'the time is shortened' (*v.* 29). But the implication is simply that it is not worth while for the unmarried to marry, whilst the married will do well to pay little

[1] Though the suggestion that this is implied even in the text of S. Matthew is contrary to the facts; *supra*, p. 68.

attention to the joys and distractions of their condition. Thus the nearness of the end is mentioned not to show that celibacy, though heroic, is *possible*, but merely that it is *wise policy*; and though the prohibition of divorce comes in the same chapter (as also the advice to widows not to remarry), this passage is entirely disconnected from the apocalyptic reference.

But whatever be the case with S. Paul's teaching, the truth about our Lord is obvious. Even if Jesus taught the immediate coming of the Kingdom, and also demanded an ascetic life of His disciples, we have no reason to infer any interior nexus between the two facts. He taught the former because it seemed true to Him; He demanded the latter because it seemed right. Hence even if we believe that He taught the forthcoming incursion of eternity into the things of time, and was mistaken in doing so, we cannot infer that He was also mistaken in advocating a far higher standard in marriage than the world has ever been ready to accept. Let us assume at most that He *may* have been mistaken in forbidding remarriage after divorce, and enquire simply whether the arguments usually advanced in its favour are sufficiently cogent to compel us to admit the truth of the view.

III

Discarding, then, for a time all appeal to the teaching of Jesus, we may ask what arguments can be advanced for the view that divorce, either at will, or on specified grounds (such as adultery), should be allowed to the Christian. This is a battlefield which has often been fought over. Briefly, however, the relevant arguments seem to be as follows.[1]

There is, first of all, the view of those who allege that marriage is a purely private contract, and that no public authority, whether Church or State, has the right to dictate its terms.[2] It is a matter for the two persons concerned, and for no one else whatever, to decide on what conditions their union shall be made or broken; and any interference with this right is wholly unwarrantable. This is a claim which, it would seem, no Church or State could very well grant, either in general, or in this particular case. For though contracts belong very much to the sphere of private law, they do nevertheless continually affect matters of public concern and well-being; and any corporate body which has the well-being of a vast number of members laid upon it as a responsibility, must claim the right, on occasion, to limit the activities of individuals for the good of the whole. Hence it is within the sphere of the State to forbid certain contracts, or types of contract, as contrary to public

[1] A further argument ('Not every couple who are married are joined together by God') is considered at the end of this chapter, *infra*, p. 123.

[2] On a minor variation of this view, which would refuse the right of discipline to the *Church*, see *infra*, p. 135.

policy, and so to pronounce them illegal; just as it is within the competence of the Church to denounce them as immoral, and exercise discipline against those who nevertheless attempt to enter into them. No one but a complete individualist would venture to contest this right.

It is contended, however, that marriage at least is a sphere in which no public interest is concerned, and that, without injury to the general principle, the community should allow individuals to enter into, and to break off, sex-relationships at will. Here, indeed, a further distinction must be observed. All serious thinkers, however far removed from the Christian tradition they may be, agree that once parenthood has supervened upon mating, the public interest is vitally affected. At *this* point, at least, legislation must have its place, determining the responsibilities of parents towards one another and towards their children, and enforcing the discharge of those responsibilities by appropriate penalties. But parenthood does not always supervene, and can to a large extent be guarded against. In such cases, it is urged, individuals are surely free to enact their own laws of ' marriage ' and ' divorce ' for themselves.

It is on the basis of this argument that the plea for free ' sex-experimentation ' during the years of adolescence, and even later, is frequently put forward even by eminent thinkers. We must recur to this view—which in effect regards sexual experience apart from the fact of parenthood as a form of harmless private recreation—at a slightly later stage. But here we can notice that in one country, at least, where 'experimentation' has gone a considerable distance, the social consequences have already proved so alarming that its regulation by law is seriously demanded. The legalization of 'companionate marriage' advocated by Judge Lindsey,[1] 'with the right to divorce by mutual consent for childless couples, usually without payment of alimony', implies that 'experimentation' has in fact produced so considerable a disturbance of public relationships that it requires definite legal control; and the phrase '*usually* without payment of alimony' suggests visions of a new branch of matrimonial law, with new courts to administer it, defining, deciding, and enforcing (as a matter of public policy) the responsibilities of those who enter into this proposed relationship. If practical proof is needed that, even in the most unbiased modern minds, 'marriage' cannot be treated as a matter of private whim and fancy, but must be viewed on the plane of public interest, even where parenthood is deliberately and successfully excluded, nothing could be more significant than Judge Lindsey's attitude.[2]

We may pass to an entirely different argument,

[1] A convenient account and discussion in J. P. Lichtenberger, *Divorce*, pp. 438–46.

[2] Further on this point, *infra*, pp. 120–3.

which at least has the merit of definiteness. It is urged in defence of the remarriage of an innocent person whose partner has been divorced for adultery, and it takes the form : 'Adultery destroys the marriage bond.' I do not know of any positive scriptural ground on which this view can be held, except an extremely unnatural interpretation of 1 Cor. 6 [15, 16]—a passage in which S. Paul can at most be understood to be showing the radical inconsistency between unchastity and the profession of Christianity, by a metaphor more forcible than exact ; and which certainly carries no such implication with it as that suggested.

Apart from this, however, two questions arise which prove the view to be entirely untenable. The first is, Why should this power of 'dissolving' a marriage be attributed to marital infidelity, and be withheld from sins in every degree as flagrant violations of the duty of husband to wife and wife to husband—persistent cruelty, or neglect or desertion, for example ? Indeed, many of these sins are very often more flagrant than adultery. An isolated act of infidelity may be the result of momentary passion or loss of self-control, but cruelty and desertion are conscious and deliberate. Surely, therefore, they must destroy the marriage-bond even more effectively than adultery is said to do ? There seems to be no satisfactory answer to this question. The view under consideration is no more than another instance of that over-emphasis on the physical, as distinct from the spiritual, aspect of marriage which has done so much harm in the past. And its supporters must consider carefully whether criticism of this character does not as a matter of fact completely invalidate it.[1]

More important, however, is the second question, even though at first sight it appears pedantic and casuistical. If adultery does indeed dissolve the marriage bond, at what moment does it do so? At the moment when it is committed—or at the moment when it is discovered by the innocent party—or at the moment when it is established as a fact after judicial enquiry? It seems unlikely that the first of these possibilities is really intended. That would mean that the world might be full at any moment of innumerable ' marriages ' that were no marriages. It would mean, furthermore, that the guilty party, who knew that he had committed adultery, although he had successfully concealed the fact from his partner, might at once contract a new marriage without doing any further wrong in the sight of God—the first marriage being already and in fact null and void by reason of his sin. And finally, it would mean that all children born to the couple after the act of adultery had been committed

[1] It may be added that the criticism in question makes it *a fortiori* incredible that, if our Lord admitted any exception to this prohibition of re-marriage after divorce, it should have been *this* exception and no other.

were *ipso facto* illegitimate (the marriage having been dissolved), and would have to be declared to be so whenever the fact was discovered and proved—even if the discovery did not take place until many years afterwards. The legal confusion which would result from the adoption of this principle, (and if morally sound, it ought to be adopted by law) would be quite incalculable.

Nor is it likely that the second possibility is seriously meant. For no civilized community in the world, whether Christian or not, would allow an 'innocent' husband or wife to separate from a partner, and marry someone else, on the mere grounds of being personally convinced that adultery had been committed. The issues involved are too tremendous for individuals to take the law into their own hands in this way; and the possibilities of error, even where evidence is sifted by an impartial court, are sufficiently great to forbid such action to be taken merely after a private enquiry by the person most directly interested. This interpretation, therefore, could be held only in the face of all educated and reasonable opinion.

Nor does criticism stop there. The interpretation in question would have a further corollary. If the marriage is at an end the moment the innocent person has discovered his or her partner's guilt, then it is wrong for the former to cohabit with the latter even for a moment longer. They are no more husband and wife. So the condonation of the offence by the forgiveness of the offender, and the resumption of matrimonial relations when penitence is shown, so far from being (as they now are in the eyes of all) not merely legitimate but also a proof of high Christian charity, become the sin of a man and woman living together without being married. Nor can such condonation be vindicated by appeal to the principle of ' renewal of consent '. That would be possible if adultery had merely made the marriage *voidable* ; but since (we are told) it has in fact dissolved it, or made it void, there is nothing left that can be revalidated by consent.

It seems then that what must be meant by this statement that ' Adultery dissolves the marriage bond ', is the very different statement, ' Adultery makes the marriage bond *voidable*, if the injured party chooses to bring an action for divorce.' So stated, we have, in effect, the present English law on the subject ; and it is urged that the Church should recognize this law and conform to it. But even so, we have not escaped from the realm of inconvenient questions. For it is natural to ask once more, ' Why should this be asserted only of adultery, and not (as in so many codes) of other causes too ? ' And to this there seems to be no satisfactory answer. If it be said that adultery is an offence, and a very grave offence, against the innocent partner, that no doubt is true. But so are cruelty, neglect and desertion ; and a man would be hard put to it to prove that the former offence stood in a graver category than these latter ones. And if, on the other hand, it be said that adultery puts the innocent party in a position of unbearable hardship, this can be alleged every bit as much not merely of cruelty, neglect, and desertion; but also of confirmed criminality, drunkenness, drug-taking and insanity. Indeed, it may well be that these latter conditions create greater hardships for the unfortunate husband and wife than does infidelity, except in cases of the most refined sensibilities.

We seem, therefore, to have reached a point of view which can only be expressed logically by saying that marriage ought to be dissoluble wherever it is proved to bring excessive hardship on either partner. This is not, indeed, quite so lax a ruling as that which would allow divorce by mutual consent. But in practice it would approximate to it; for it would be supremely easy for a couple who wished to be rid of one another to provide evidence of hardship suffered by one at least of them. The issue is therefore clear. As against the traditional position, 'Marriage ought never, by the nature of things, to be dissolved,' there is arrayed a body of opinion which denies its truth; and in comparison with this issue the subordinate question, 'If marriage is not by nature indissoluble, on what grounds can it legitimately be dissolved?' is of secondary importance. It remains, therefore, to ask the clear question, Is the Christian tradition in this matter any longer capable of defence?

IV

For various reasons, into which we need not enter, the world is no longer susceptible to any argument which alleges that such-and-such a principle is the ' invariable tradition ' of the Church. It is even sceptical and unmoved if it is told that the principle is unquestionably one which Jesus Himself enunciated. It appeals to reason, and to reason only. Even so, it is suspicious of syllogistic argument, and is inclined to believe that the conclusions are usually contained somehow or other in the premisses. Hence it is not to be expected that any argument, however valid, will carry immediate conviction with those who are unwilling to be convinced. This, however, does not exonerate the Christian from attempting to examine matters of debate impartially and rationally; nor does it mean that a valid argument will in the end fail to carry conviction, when its weight has had time in which to make itself felt. It becomes the duty of every Christian therefore—and indeed of every serious man, of whatever religious persuasion he may be—to examine the marriage problem and seek such light as reason can throw upon it. The following suggestions are no more than a contribution towards such consideration.

Any continuous activity or occupation upon which a man enters appears to belong by nature to one of three categories; and if it is assigned, in any particular case, to the inappropriate category, its moral purposes will neither be understood nor fulfilled. Many occupations, indeed, find a place in more than one of these categories—perhaps, strictly speaking, all of them do—and so our attitude towards them is complex. But each category has its own rules, and it is not impossible to find the proper priority of these rules where two categories, or even three, overlap. A continuous activity or occupation, then, must be either an *employment*, or a *recreation*, or a *vocation*. It may be more than one of these ; indeed the greatest natural happiness is that of the man who finds in one and the same occupation both his employment, and his recreation, and his vocation. But to make this clear, a little more explanation is needed.

By an *employment* we mean the activity whereby a man earns his living. A *recreation* is an activity or occupation which he takes up for the pleasure that it gives him. A *vocation* is one in which he recognizes, or ought to recognize, that God has laid upon him obligations to be discharged. The difference of attitude we adopt towards the three is as follows. An employment (in so far as it is an employment only, and not a recreation or a vocation as well) we are free to lay aside the moment it has fulfilled its purpose of providing for our daily needs. A recreation again, in so far as it is merely a recreation,[1] we are at liberty to lay aside

[1] Many recreations (e.g. any kind of team-game) carry obligations with them, both towards other members of the team, and

the moment we cease to take pleasure in it. Once again, it has fulfilled its purpose, or is fulfilling it no longer; and we have neither need nor use for it further. In both these cases, no duty is laid upon us to do otherwise. But where an occupation is a vocation (be it a vocation only, or a recreation or an employment as well) it is obviously our duty not to abandon it so long as it may be believed to be God's will that we should remain in it.

To which of these three categories does 'marriage'—or indeed the sex-life in general—belong? No one nowadays will hold that it is by nature an employment—a means of earning a living. We are told that the Victorian woman regarded it in such a light; and the same would appear to have been true of the Victorian man as well. At all events, Mr. Trollope's heroes assess their own values in the marriage market as frankly as do Miss Austen's heroines; and one of the most famous of the Victorians, Mr. Bumble, recapitulated his connubial experience in the words:—'I sold myself for six teaspoons, a pair of sugar tongs and a milk pot, with a small quantity of second-

towards opponents—in particular the obligation to go on with the game for an agreed length of time, and to play it according to agreed rules. In this respect they are of the nature of vocations as well as recreations. But a *mere* recreation which carries no such obligations (as, for example, reading a novel, solving a puzzle, smoking a pipe, or playing yo-yo) can obviously be laid on one side as soon as it ceases to please.

hand furniture, and twenty pound in money. I went very reasonable. Cheap—dirt cheap!'[1]

However, the view that in essence the sex-life is for either man or woman a means of earning a livelihood is not likely to find many serious champions. On the other hand, the view that it is of the nature of a recreation, and that no blame attaches to those who treat it as such, could scarcely be more popular than it is to-day among the unthinking and irresponsible. We have already seen, however, that the results of this view in the United States have caused quite impartial observers, who cannot in any way be accused of a bias towards traditionalism, to demand that the recreation should be regulated by law. This in itself is a piece of evidence of vast importance. But more important still is the consideration that there are some things so dangerous in their consequences, that neither society as a whole, nor any part of it, may be allowed to treat them as toys. There was a time—it is still misnamed the 'age of chivalry'—when warlike pursuits were the recreation of the nobility and gentry; and the world has only in our own day reached the conclusion that war is not a game, and that no one must be allowed to treat it as such, because the consequences of such an attitude are too disastrous to be endured any longer.

A cynic might find grounds for laughter in the fact that the same epoch, which has seen the final

[1] *Oliver Twist*, ch. 37.

condemnation of the view that war is a game, should witness the spectacle of a world falling over itself to play at the game of sex. But what is true of the one is true of the other. The passions released by irresponsible surrender to the sex-instinct are as violent, far-reaching and terrifying in their ultimate consequences as those released by militarism. A man must be utterly deaf to the warnings both of history and of psychology to contemplate with equanimity the thought of a society in which sex is treated primarily as a means of personal amusement. There may perhaps be those sufficiently self-controlled to play the game with restraint for a while; but who is there who can honestly say of himself that, *if he were to treat sex solely as a recreation*, he could keep its solicitations within bounds? And if once this view of what sex stands for gained general currency, and were endorsed by State and Church as well, is any-one imaginative enough to predict the horrors that would in time ensue? [1]

We are left then with the conclusion that the only way in which the mating of man and woman can properly be regarded is as a vocation. This has, perhaps, been said so often that it is no more than a truism. But if we realize that it is of the

[1] It may be added that a dispassionate review of the testimony of those who have consistently treated sex as a recreation does not lead to the conclusion that they have found it either edifying, inspiring, or satisfying. Cf. W. Lippmann, *Preface to Morals*, pp. 302–5.

essence of a vocation that it should not be treated as though it were merely an employment or a recreation, the truism comes to life once more, and carries with it consequences of vital importance. Marriage is a vocation, because in it a man and a woman are called upon by God to serve one another in every way that is possible, and to serve their children, as well, if God gives them parenthood. In this service, then, each must continue so long as there is any chance that it is God's will for them, and regardless of any failure of the other to return the equal service that is due ; for the essence of a vocation (as distinct from an employment or a recreation) is that its term is set not by what can be received from it, but by what can be given in it. Thus the phrase ' till death us do part ', and no other phrase, expresses properly the true duration of marriage. The unfaithful partner may repent, the absentee may return, the moral degenerate may be converted, the invalid—even though he does not recover—may be grateful for care and affection. If I am not ready and waiting to play my part at such times, I have failed in the task that God has given me.

To this argument it might very well be replied : ' I admit that marriage is in essence a vocation. But I doubt whether it is God's will that I should invariably continue in any vocation in which there is only a distant possibility of my being of further use, whilst I see another vocation open to me in which I am certain that I could do true and valuable service. Thus if my present partner, A, deserts me for another, and so makes my chance of giving further service infinitely remote, whilst I know that I could make B's life far more happy and effective than it is at present—surely it would be not merely legitimate, but even right, for me to secure a divorce from A and marry B? Would not the very facts be themselves a sign that God had released me from my first obligation, to require of me new service in another union?'

At first sight this criticism seems unanswerable. God does often call men and women to a change of vocation. We do not blame the schoolmaster, let us say, who abandons his teaching for the purpose of entering the priesthood, under the sure conviction that he can do God better service in the latter capacity than in the former. Yet the argument misses a point of supreme importance. Marriage is a vocation of a very special character. Its nature is that of a personal allegiance, deliberately assumed, to a second person. Looking at the matter from an impartial standpoint, Church and State alike speak of the exchange of marriage vows as a 'contract'. But, if we are right in thinking of marriage as a 'vocation to an allegiance', then, in the estimation of the two persons concerned, the vows should have the force of an *unconditional promise*—a promise to 'love, comfort, honour, and keep' the chosen partner, regardless of any barriers that may arise between them. It is of the essence of such a promise that, even though the person to whom it has been made professes to give a release from it, this fact does not in itself constitute a release; no more does the fact of an apparent opportunity of making a similar promise to another person, who seems at the moment to have a greater need of it, if such a second promise can only be made (as in this case) at the expense of breaking the first.

For this, surely, is what is meant by true allegiance or loyalty. The Old Testament portrayed it in Ruth's devotion to Naomi, and David's refusal to 'stretch forth his hand' against Saul, 'the Lord's anointed'. The Greek world knew it, and celebrated it in the fables of Psyché and Cupid, and Penelope and Odysseus. The Christian world has known it, and expressed it in countless ballads and romances. In one form or another, such loyalty was Shakespeare's dearest theme—the loyalty of Viola to the duke who ignored her love; the loyalty of Hermione to the husband who had loaded her with dishonour; the loyalty of Cordelia to the father, and of Kent to the master, who had cast them off. In every case the patient waiting for a further opportunity of service seemed purposeless and vain. But that did not affect the quality of the allegiance; and none of the loyal souls concerned entered upon any course which would preclude them from discharging the duties which they had assumed, if the miracle of opportunity should present itself once more.

Here we touch the root of the matter. When all questions of mere self-pleasing have been set aside, the essential difficulty for which divorce is demanded as a remedy is not the adultery, cruelty, or desertion by which the 'guilty' partner offends against the 'innocent' partner. For such difficulties separation would be a sufficient remedy. *The true difficulty begins only when the 'innocent' partner meets someone else whom he or she desires to marry.* It may be that this meeting only takes place after long-continued offence by the 'guilty' partner. It may be that the 'desire to marry' is a genuine and disinterested desire to serve within the marriage-relationship. But the fact remains that the innocent partner can only think of marriage with this third person as possible, if he or she is prepared to disown the original allegiance—to play traitor to one of the most solemn obligations which anyone can undertake. Once we recognize that the vocation of marriage carries with it this special duty of personal and unconditional loyalty, to enter upon a second marriage during the lifetime of the first partner—whatever tragedy the former union may have involved; whatever possibilities of devoted service the latter may offer—must be adjudged a fatal decline from the ideal. And it is with the ideal alone that at the moment we are concerned.

It may, of course, be possible to imagine an

extreme case in which it would seem that all hope of the loyal partner being of further service must be finally excluded, even though death has not separated the couple. But the case would have to be a very extreme one, and consequently very rare—far more rare than the innumerable 'hard cases' for which the redress of divorce is always being demanded. And even in such an extreme case there would be good grounds for urging that the obligation of indissolubility still held. For in all but the most extreme instances it holds unquestionably (whatever the world may say); and where this is true of any principle of real importance, a society is within its rights in demanding its acceptance by all its members, that no one may be able to plead for an exception to be made in his case, on the ground that it has been made in others which he will only too readily believe to be no more tragic than his own.

V

With these considerations in mind, we may revert to the argument which alleged that a man and woman should be left free to contract together for the purpose of cohabitation on any terms which might be agreed upon between them. We have already seen reason to reject this argument as a general plea; but we can now go further. For if the union of man and woman can only fulfil its purpose when it is regarded as a vocation—and a vocation of a very special character—by each of the parties, then the Church is surely right in discountenancing anything which would prevent them from looking upon it in that light, or suiting their attitude and actions to this view. A given couple may, indeed, contract to marry one another mainly for the ' recreation ' which they hope the adventure will afford. They may in addition regard it as a contract for the ' employment ' of one of them by the other—as a wife discharges the duties of a housekeeper towards her husband in return for board, lodging, and clothing. And if these were the only ends of matrimony they would be free to set whatever term they agreed upon to the original contract.

But to regard marriage as either employment or recreation, or both together, and no more, is, as we have seen, to prostitute it to base uses, and to ignore its essential character as a vocation of allegiance. It may be that in a given marriage neither partner will ever reach a spiritual standpoint which will enable them to see it in this, its true, light. It may be that only one of them will do so. But so long as they are forbidden to set a limit to the duration of the contract, the possibility of discovering it to be a vocation will not be excluded. Indeed, the very fact of the prohibition may suggest the reason why it is being maintained. If, on the other hand, the duration of the contract is allowed to be limited, or made terminable at short notice, or in certain eventualities, the whole psychological background will have been changed; and the one safeguard removed which, at moments of danger, might keep the couple together, and preserve the possibility of realizing the ideal.

From the same angle we can deal with another suggestion which is often made, in language more popular than exact. "Those whom God has truly joined together, man has not the right to put asunder," is quoted; with the significant addition, 'But there are very many couples, even of those married in church, who have obviously not been joined together by God.' It would be interesting to know the tests by which the supporters of this argument decide whether a marriage has been made by God or not. Shall we say that God did not join the couple together, if one or both of them appear to have entered the union with less than a due sense of responsibility? Or will it be proof that God was not the matchmaker, if one or both of the parties fall short of a certain specified standard of marital devotion after the ceremony has taken place? Are we to accept the evidence of the parties themselves, or the verdict of a civil court, as final in determining the divine responsibility in the matter? Or must the Church have a forum of her own to decide?

These are not flippant enquiries; each one of them demands an answer. But in strict truth, both enquiries and answers are irrelevant once we accept the implications of the idea that marriage is a vocation. There are many courses of action upon which a man enters lightly and almost casually, which bring him face to face with the stern demands of duty before the end; his irresponsibility at the outset does not mean that God has no work for him to do in the path he has chosen to tread. There are many who have vocations—just as there are many who have duties—of which so far they realize nothing. Our business is not to say to them, 'If you think you have no duty here, then you *have* no duty'—a foolish and meaningless remark [1]—but to help them to discover wherein their duty or vocation lies. There are many who fail in carrying out the demands of their vocations, either wilfully or through ignorance; there are many who find their vocations beset by almost insuperable difficulties and almost overwhelming sorrows. But none of these things affect the fact that a vocation is a vocation, and that its requirements must be satisfied if men and women are to lead the good life.

All this is as true of marriage as of any other vocation. If God allows a man and woman to be joined together in matrimony, He calls each of them to a life of unremitting service in the other's regard. The fact that they were deaf to that call at the outset, or have grown deaf to it since, does not for a moment entitle us to say that from this

[1] See my *Threshold of Ethics*, ch. 5.

even if by accident alone, the primitive and Catholic principle that the essence of marriage consists in the full and free consent of the two persons concerned; and so made it possible for the Church to envisage the whole question once more in its true perspective.

In theory, therefore, the Church of England is admirably placed for expounding the true principles of Christian marriage. In actual fact, her position is not so satisfactory. She stands alone, indeed, among the great communions of the Christian world, in possessing no recognized safety valve for 'hard cases' in matrimony. Canon 107 of 1603, which is still authoritative for us, prescribes as follows:—

"In all sentences pronounced for divorce[1] and separation *a thoro et mensâ*, there shall be a caution and restraint inserted in the act of the said sentence that the parties so separated shall live chastely and continently; neither shall they, during each other's life, contract matrimony with any other person. And for the better observation of this last clause, the said sentences of divorce shall not be pronounced until the party or parties requiring the same have given good and sufficient caution and security into the court, that they will not in any way break or transgress the said restraint or prohibition."

This canon is, of course, wholly inoperative to-

[1] 'Divorce' here, of course, means 'separation' only; *supra*, p. 48.

day; for ecclesiastical jurisdiction in matrimonial causes has fallen into desuetude as a result of secular legislation arrogating all such jurisdiction for the King's Courts alone.[1] But it is something that the Church of England should still possess clear documentary evidence of her view as to the indissolubility of marriage. On the other hand, there is one respect in which nineteenth-century legislation has affected her position vitally. The Church now lives in a State in which divorce and remarriage are allowed by civil law on certain specified grounds; and there is strong social pressure brought upon her to recognize by formal pronouncement that remarriage after such divorce is not in every case sinful. If she were to submit to this pressure, her course would for the present at least be simple. But she would be faced with the fact that it might be no more than a temporary expedient, and an expedient, moreover, which for the sake of a moment's breathing-space involved the sacrifice of an essential principle.

For it is unlikely that either secular legislation or the temper of society will become more rigorous in regard to marriage questions, and a time may come when they will be considerably more lax. 'Hard cases' are created by other causes besides marital infidelity; and there is no reason to sup-

[1] Divorce Act, 1857. There is no doubt that the Church acquiesced in this innovation; but it has not of course surrendered its right to revive its own courts if it should wish to do so.

pose that a State, which already allows legal remarriage to a 'guilty' *divorcé*, will not, sooner or later, take the step of allowing it in far more deserving cases. This would mean that in due course the demand for divorce, with the right of remarriage, on the ground of a partner's insanity, or habitual criminality, or confirmed alcoholism, would prove successful; and no one can say that, in view of the enormous concession already made in the case of the 'guilty' partner, any of these permissions would be other than equitable. Even 'mental cruelty' or 'mutual incompatibility' might come in time to be recognized as a sufficient ground for divorce in English law, as in some other modern codes. For any Christian Church to acquiesce in such a moral landslide would be intolerable; and the divergence between civil permission and ecclesiastical prohibition, when it comes, is bound to precipitate a conflict. But the longer the Church hesitates to assert her right to determine for her own members the limits beyond which she will not recognize them as being truly married, the more difficult will it be for her to adopt an independent position when the final conflict comes.

Thus even if it be alleged that the present demands of society are such as the Church might without disaster concede, there is still the future to be considered. Many churchmen would take the view: 'There seems to be no demand on the part of society as a whole that a person remarried after being divorced for adultery should be admitted to communion: there *is* a demand that the remarried "innocent" party should be admitted. Why not, therefore, concede this second demand? Even so, our system would be stricter than that of the eastern Churches, which allow divorce and remarriage to their members on many other grounds besides that of a partner's adultery; so there can be no danger of betraying a Catholic principle.' But the danger remains the same as before. A concession which might conceivably be granted, if it were known to be a final one, becomes a source of weakness if there is no guarantee that others more serious still will not be demanded. Sooner or later the Church may have to call a halt, and in consequence we have two questions to consider: (1) How can she call a halt? and (2) Where should it be called?

II

The first question opens up the entire problem of the relations existing not merely between the Church and the State, but also between the Church and that more indefinable entity which we call 'public opinion'. At the moment the Church of England has neither the coherence nor the machinery to enable her to take effective action in this, or indeed in many other matters. Her members are many of them members by convention or convenience alone. They are often ignorant of much for which she stands: almost as often they are sceptical as to the truth of much which she asserts. If we are to be frank with ourselves, we must admit that there are few practical matters on which, at the moment, the Church could call for corporate action by her members with any reasonable hope of a coherent or enthusiastic response. And if she were to attempt to re-establish a system of discipline over her members with a view to securing greater unity of self-consciousness, and something like an effective corporate will, it is certain that she would be faced not merely by external opposition, but also by internal dissension of the most alarming kind.

It is possible, of course, that the growing indifference of society as a whole to ecclesiastical affairs, together with a domestic movement in the English Church for the better education of Anglicans in the principles of their religion, might in time remove these difficulties. Even so we should still have to recognize that the civil courts, as the law now runs, so far from sustaining any independent jurisdiction of the Church over the laity who profess allegiance to her, are likely to frown severely upon any attempt to revive such ecclesiastical discipline. It seems clear, therefore, that in view of the possibility of grave clashes between the Christian tradition and the law of England on the marriage question at no very distant date, the Church cannot afford to let the matter of her independent jurisdiction over her members remain in a state of suspended animation. It may be a long time before legislation recognizes the principle for which it seems we are bound to contend; but no one who is alert to the dangers which surround the Church can be excused from the task of attempting to secure general benevolence towards the principle which is at stake.

What is needed is a recognition by the legislature that membership in the Church of England is to some extent contractual—that is, that no one can expect to receive the privileges of membership without conforming to the conditions, and discharging the obligations, of membership. To some slight extent, perhaps, this is the case at present. It is doubtful, for example, whether a civil action would lie against a parish priest for refusing to recite the English burial office at the funeral of an unbaptized person; or for refusing communion to one who, while professing to be a member of the Church of England,[1] was neither confirmed nor ready and desirous to be confirmed. The principle is also recognized by the franchise qualifications under the Enabling Act. But in these matters we are only touching the fringe of the

[1] This qualification must be added; for the courts might take the view which finds favour in some circles that the rubric in question refers only to professed members of the Church of England.

real problem. The ideal to be aimed at must be that the Church shall have the right to require of her members conformity to certain conditions; and to refuse them the benefits of sacraments if they refuse to comply—always provided that the conditions in question do not violate the rights of citizens or the principles of natural justice. If this were recognized, the status of the Church of England would, in one respect at least, be raised to the level of the remainder of the Anglican communion throughout the world.

Hand in hand with this would have to come the recognition that the powers of self-legislation at present available to the Church—whether through the Convocations or through the Church Assembly—are wholly inadequate for her real needs. Neither in this respect nor in the former is it possible for us to consider here what steps would be necessary before either result could be secured. It is notorious that any advance in these directions will meet with strenuous opposition. But nothing is more evident than that, until public opinion has been educated to recognize at once the equity and the expediency of satisfying these claims for the Church, we shall remain in an uneasy transition period, in which it will be all but impossible to employ even the mildest disciplinary action to enforce our witness to principle. It is at least arguable that this inactivity to which the Church is at present condemned is slowly but surely sapping her powers of ultimate recovery. This means that the ecclesiastical statesman who in other spheres is working for the emancipation of the Church from the superior control of the State, has a double task even in the matter of marriage. As a standard at which to aim, he has to consider how he would wish the Church to act if she were free to live her own life; whilst as an immediate and temporary expedient, he has to make up his mind as to the action which should be taken (if any be possible at all) with regard to marriage, in the actual circumstances which at present hedge the Church about.

III

We may take first the question of ultimate standard. Assume, *per impossibile*, that within the next few years the Church of England were able to regulate her own life, as regards both legislation and discipline, without fear of external interference. How should she deal with the marriage problem? Those who maintain that divorce, with the right to remarriage, is in certain cases wholly accordant with the mind of Christ, would of course insist that no ecclesiastical action should in any way violate this principle. But the view in question is one which we have seen cause to reject. New Testament tradition and the argument from reason alike appear to invalidate it. What alternatives, then, are possible?

First of all, and in a class by itself, there is the suggestion that it is the business of the Church only to state ideals, but never to attempt to enforce them by discipline. The argument is often presented from two different angles. On the one hand, it is said, to refuse the sacraments to anyone, on any occasion, is to 'usurp the prerogatives of God'. On the other hand, we are told that in the conditions of the modern Church of England everyone who asks to receive communion may unhesitatingly be assumed to be in 'good faith' —that is, to have a conscience void of offence in all things—and that from such persons the sacraments should never on any account be withheld, however much they may diverge from the Church's rule of conduct.

Now although the first of these arguments is theological in form, and can be met theologically, the premise upon which both of them depend is that civilized men and women do not differ very much in their genuine estimates of 'right' and 'wrong'. Such a view derives wholly from a too limited experience of the infinite varieties of moral psychology. The majority of civilized men and women are, no doubt, as conventional in their ethical outlook as in anything else. But the exceptions to this rule are very numerous; and as a matter of fact there is no principle of conduct, be it never so crazy, perverse, or outrageous, that cannot be and has not been professed (to all appearances in good faith) by persons claiming in many instances to be Christians, and in every case brought up in the atmosphere of Christian civilization. The conscientious polygamist, for example, has existed in England within our own time: and it is not difficult to imagine him both practising and preaching polygamy in the name of religion. What would happen, then, if such a known advocate of polygamy claimed membership in the Church of England, and asked for the sacraments without in any way abating his public campaign for the recognition of his doctrine as a genuinely Christian ideal? It is unlikely that anyone would say that he ought to receive them because his convictions were held in good faith (as we have assumed them to be), or would accuse those who withheld them from him of usurping the prerogatives of God.

If this is so, it would seem that anyone who maintains that the Church has no right to exercise discipline over those who claim to be her members has never really thought out the implications of his position. We shall not go far astray if we assume that to most people, if they have given the matter more than passing attention, this right is so obvious in principle that no argument is needed to enforce it.

But the question of the nature of the discipline to be exercised in the particular case of the remarriage of divorced persons is a very perplexing one. The most obvious view is that no concession whatever should be made to the hardness of men's hearts. Any member of the Church who remarried, during the lifetime of the first partner, whether after securing a divorce or being divorced, should be refused communion until such time as he or she separated from this second 'partner'. If we accept the conclusion previously reached that as a matter of historic fact our Lord actually forbade remarriage after divorce in any circumstances, this would at first sight seem to render the suggested course of action inevitable. But the conclusion does not follow. For, emphatic and unequivocal though we have seen His words to be, they do not prescribe any specific course of action to the Church. They state the 'law', but say nothing as to the 'sanctions' by which it is to be enforced. Thus if it could be shown that in all probability the universal observance of this 'law' throughout the world could best be secured by other measures than the excommunication of those who contravened it, we should have good ground for rejecting this alternative, and should have no reason to suppose that in doing so we were being disloyal to the Church's Founder.[1]

Alternatively, there is the view that some concession ought to be made. The concession usually suggested is that the so-called 'innocent'

[1] The same considerations might be regarded as offering a possible way of escape from the dilemma referred to, *supra*, p. 38.

party to a divorce suit should be allowed to re-marry without forfeiting his or her right to communion. Of the logic of this concession, as it stands, we must say more in a moment. The support which it has secured is evidenced by the fact that it is the view implied in the resolutions of successive Lambeth Conferences since 1888. Nor can it be said that the bishops approved of the concession simply as a temporary measure necessitated by the present servitude of the Church in England. For on the one hand, the resolutions in which it is embodied envisage many branches of the Anglican communion which are as free from secular interference as any Church in Christendom. And on the other hand, the resolutions of the 1908 and 1930 Conferences on the subject contemplate *some* legislative changes at least before they can be put into practical effect in this country. The recommendation, for example, that 'the marriage of one whose former partner is still living should not be celebrated in Church' assumes that the clergy have a control over their churches and services which as a matter of fact is not at present theirs by law; since the Divorce Act of 1857 only allows a parish priest to refuse to celebrate the marriage of a parishioner where the latter has been divorced for his or her adultery: and even so requires him to lend his church for the purpose if any other clergyman can be found to perform the ceremony.

The Lambeth recommendations, then, were not specifically drafted with an eye to the actual circumstances of the Church in England; and it may be assumed that the imaginary circumstances which they had in view were of such a character that the Church would be free, within all reasonable limits, to grant or to withhold privileges from her members, without regard to anything except the due discharge of her spiritual mission.

Here, then, are the two practical alternatives in their simplest forms. It is obvious that the choice between them is a matter of the greatest difficulty. For this reason, we cannot but be surprised that the 1930 resolutions (which, as we have seen, envisage the circumstances of an enfranchised Church) speak as though there were no choice at all. They have no hesitation in putting forward their concessions; they never even consider the possibility that the course of concession is the wrong course. The 1888 Conference did, indeed, discover a reason for concession in 'the fact that there had always been a difference of opinion in the Church on the question whether our Lord meant to forbid marriage to the innocent party in a divorce for adultery'. This, it must be admitted, is at best weak ground on which to have acted; for the right course, where there is a difference of opinion between authorities on an ethical matter of vital importance, is obviously to attempt to decide which opinion has the more weight behind it; not to adopt the laxer opinion without further question. But the 1930 resolution is even more casual in the matter. It gives no reason for concession at all. It assumes that concession is either inevitable or unexceptionable.

If, however, we are considering the position of a communion free from vexatious secular interference, it becomes very doubtful whether concession is the right course. Compromise on a point of principle is always a dangerous expedient; it can only be justified as the lesser of two evils. In such problems every man must estimate the arguments for and against each alternative for himself; all that anyone else can do for him is to help him to realize the relevant considerations. Not one of those who accept the view that our Lord forbade remarriage after divorce in every case, but will hesitate long before embracing the side of concession. Even if he ultimately decides that it is the lesser of the two evils involved, the conclusion will be a very bitter one to him. Nevertheless, though it be a conclusion from which we all shrink, and which we shall not accept without the most earnest discussion and consideration, we must recognize that the arguments against the other alternative—the course of 'no compromise'—are very weighty too.

There is first the argument from history. The vast majority of Christian bodies have found it necessary, sooner or later, to provide some safety-valve for the pent-up instincts which rebelled against the rigid rule of primitive days. We may deplore the fact, but it remains a fact nevertheless. And we cannot deny that this is one of the reasons, perhaps, why they were able to tame the unruly passions of the heathen races with which they came into contact. They tempered the wind to the shorn lamb, and so made the gradual acceptance of the Christian code more possible than it would otherwise have been. It is true, of course, that the Church of England, without any such recognized safety-valve, has also managed to keep its head above the waves of secularism. But we cannot quote the Church of England as in practice a representative of the primitive system. The popular tolerance of the remarriage of divorced persons, the conflict of opinions within the Church, the absence of effective discipline not merely over the laity, but in many respects over the clergy as well, and the constant shifting of population, have made it the simplest thing in the world for persons whom in theory the Church might be expected to excommunicate to receive the sacraments as and when they wish. The Church of England has her safety-valve; but it is no more creditable than any other, because it is the safety-valve of *laissez-faire*.

Second, we must reckon with the argument from probability. I have tried to show elsewhere [1] that a cast-iron and tyrannical discipline is almost

[1] *The Vision of God*, *pass.*; cp. especially pp. 468, 469.

inevitably bound to over-reach itself. Either it produces hypocrisy and evasion on a vast scale, or else the body which exercises it shrinks gradually to the dimensions of a tiny Puritan sect—an academy of eccentrics—whose influence upon the moral well-being of society as a whole is negligible. No one would wish to see the Church of England reduced to this position. The choice therefore is a critical one. On the one hand there is the nightmare vision of a Church adhering firmly to the purity of its full ideals, yet with an appeal which (by reason of its rigid demands) is likely to be effective only in the most limited circles; and with adherents who, because of the anti-social habits forced upon them by their convictions, are isolated from sympathetic contact with society as a whole. The other alternative is that of a Church which by politic mitigation of its ideal requirements is making its influence for good felt far beyond its own borders, but which is always haunted by the fear that its 'nature' is becoming

> 'subdued
> To what it works in, like the dyer's hand.'

As with every choice between two grave evils, so here the Christian will only decide after earnest prayer, and he will extend the fullest possible sympathy and understanding to those who, with the interests of the Church as much at heart as himself, decide in the opposite sense to his own.

Perhaps the most that can be said is this. Since the passing of the Divorce Act of 1857, the Church of England has never even attempted to experiment with what most of us would call the more heroic policy—that of adhering to the rigour of the prohibition against remarriage in any circumstances. That policy may be the wrong one—the apparently heroic often is. But ought we not to work for a state of things in which at least the experiment can be tried, before we allow ourselves to believe that even in the most favourable circumstances it is doomed to failure?

IV

Assuming, however, that it is decided that the interests of the gospel necessitate some concession to human frailty, it still remains to consider what form that concession should take. There is common agreement that the eastern Churches have capitulated too far in the matter of divorce—their own theologians and canonists do not hesitate to admit it.[1] On the other hand, any such evasion as that by which the west has from time to time impressed the principle of nullity to subserve the ends for which divorce is commonly demanded is wholly repugnant to English ideas. We can best approach the question from the point of view of the Lambeth resolutions, which imply that an 'innocent' party to a divorce suit, who has there-

[1] *Supra*, p. 52.

after married again, shall be eligible for communion, whereas a guilty party shall not.

It must be observed that this concession is accompanied by a restriction. Resolution 4 of the Conference of 1888 stated emphatically: 'Under no circumstances ought the guilty party . . . to be regarded, during the lifetime of the innocent party, as a fit recipient of the blessing of the Church on marriage.' Nothing was said as to the innocent party. But in the Conference of 1908 the following resolution [1] was carried by a majority of 3 in a house of 171:—'When an innocent person has, by means of a court of law, divorced a spouse for adultery, and desires to enter into another contract of marriage, it is undesirable that such a contract should receive the blessing of the Church.' The two recommendations are fused into one in resolution 11 (*a*) of 1930:—'The Conference, while passing no judgment on the practice of regional or national Churches within our communion, recommends that the marriage of one, whose former partner is still living, should not be celebrated according to the rites of the Church.' No suggestion is contained in the Report that this resolution was in any degree an occasion of controversy.

It might at first sight appear that, if a suggestion for the exclusion of the innocent party from remarriage in church could not be put forward at

[1] No. 40.

all in 1888, was passed only by a bare majority in 1908, and excited no controversy in 1930, the Anglican communion, so far from relaxing her marriage discipline, is tending to stiffen it. This, however, is an unwarranted inference. No such social stigma attaches to 'register office marriages' to-day as was the case twenty, and still more forty, years ago. Hence, in the public view, a resolution which in 1888 would have appeared drastic in the extreme is nowadays a matter of relative indifference. Nevertheless, we can at least say that the bishops at Lambeth have taken the opportunity of changing social conditions to give some kind of practical expression to their sense that the re-marriage of divorced persons is in some measure contrary to the mind of Christ.

The restriction, therefore, is admirable in intention. If it is to be criticized at all, its critics will only be those who hold that the penalty (once more in view of modern social conditions) is of too trivial a character to make much impression on the social conscience. We come, therefore, to the more important and more controversial suggestion. In 1888 (endorsed in 1908) it ran as follows :—

'That, recognizing the fact that there has always been a difference of opinion in the Church on the question whether our Lord meant to forbid marriage to the innocent party in a divorce for adultery, the Conference recommends that the clergy should not be instructed to refuse the sacraments or other privileges of the

Church to those who, under civil sanction, are thus married.'[1]

In 1930 this took the form :—' Where an innocent person has remarried under civil sanction and desires to receive the Holy Communion, (the Conference) recommends that the case should be referred for consideration to the bishop, subject to provincial regulations.'

In the change of expression between 1888 and 1930, we notice a real advance from a laxer to a stricter position. The 1888 Conference would apparently have frowned upon any bishop who, either generally or in a particular case, instructed his clergy to refuse the sacraments to an innocent party. The 1930 Conference leaves the individual bishop free to take this course if he think fit, subject always to provincial regulations. Nevertheless, even the 1930 resolution must encourage remarried innocent parties to expect that their request for communion will not be refused. It is to be noticed, incidentally, that the 1888 and 1908 Conferences made it clear that no concession in advance of the one under consideration would be made by the Church, however widely the civil law of divorce might be extended :—

' Inasmuch as our Lord's words expressly forbid divorce, except in the case of fornication or adultery, the Christian Church cannot recognize divorce in any other than the excepted case, or give any sanction to the

[1] Resolution 4 (*c*) of 1888 (39 of 1908).

marriage of any person who has been divorced contrary to this law, during the life of the other person.'

It is a matter for surprise and regret that the 1930 resolutions contain no statement to the same effect.

The real problem about the proposed concession is that it appears to be based upon no recognizable principle. The 1888 Conference, as has already been mentioned, attempted to vindicate it by an appeal to 'the fact that there has always been a difference of opinion in the Church on the question whether our Lord meant to forbid marriage to the innocent party'. This 'always', however, is an overstatement so startling that one is shocked to meet with it in an official document. As we have seen, there was no 'difference of opinion' as to our Lord's teaching on the point in the first six centuries—the centuries to which the Church of England has always made particular appeal. The exceptive clauses in S. Matthew were never once quoted in favour of the laxer view, but were always interpreted, not without difficulty, in favour of the sterner one. And whatever may have been the case in 1888, scholars of to-day are perhaps more unanimous that these texts (whatever their provenance) do not embody an authentic tradition of our Lord's teaching, than they are on any other point of New Testament criticism.

This suggestion having failed, we look in vain for any other to take its place. The recommendation does not accord with eastern practice; for here persons who have received a divorce on other grounds besides their partner's infidelity to the married vow are admitted to communion on remarriage; and the same privilege is extended to the guilty husband, provided that he does not marry the partner of his guilt. It does not accord with English civil law, which puts the 'innocent' and 'guilty' parties on the same footing as regards remarriage. It does not satisfy reason, since (as we have seen) there are other 'hard cases' beside that of the 'innocent party', which deserve equal consideration, and are only out of the picture at the moment because English law has not extended to them the latitude which it has allowed in the case of infidelity. Yet the 1888 and 1908 resolutions must be interpreted to mean that, even if the law allowed divorce and remarriage in these cases, it would be the duty of the Church to refuse communion. And, finally, the word 'innocent' is question-begging. For if the Church, having at present no jurisdiction of her own, is to accept the verdict of the civil courts on the facts as final, then neither partner to a divorce suit has been adjudged 'innocent'. The so-called 'innocent' persons are merely those who have successfully secured a divorce from their partners, their success being in part due to the fact that no counter-charge of adultery has been brought against them, or (if it has been brought) has been sustained by sufficient evidence.

The case is no more satisfactory if we consider the position of the 'guilty' party who has been divorced. It is implied in the resolutions that it will be fruitless for him to ask for communion if he remarries. Once again, this is not identical with eastern practice, but that is not a point of overwhelming significance. Here our difficulties are in part due to want of information. The bishops have not indicated what line of action they would propose to take in this matter. It may be said at once that no objection could be taken to the exclusion from communion of the *impenitent* adulterer, whether he married again or not.[1] But what are we to say if he shows effective signs of repentance for his original guilt, and in the end receives absolution both from the 'sin' and from the 'censure'—the excommunication with which his sin may be supposed to have been visited?

Apart from one consideration, he would seem to be entitled, on due repentance, to exactly the same treatment as the 'innocent' party. In that case it would be better if the 1930 resolution were

[1] It is to be supposed that this is the meaning of a sentence in the Archbishop of York's discussion of the 1930 resolution (*Thoughts on some Problems of the Day*, p. 51): 'The guilty party is excommunicated for his guilt, quite apart from his remarriage.' The only other interpretation would be that the writer wished to revert to the tyrannical discipline which the Church discarded at the end of the second century, whereby adultery, murder and apostasy were treated as 'unforgivable sins'; and anyone guilty of them (however great his penitence) was excluded from communion for life.

rewritten in some such form as the following :—'When a divorced person has remarried under civil sanction and, *not being on other grounds liable to ex-communication*, desires to receive the Holy Communion . . .' But the consideration to which allusion has just been made is important. It might reasonably be urged that infidelity to the marriage bond is a matter of such gravity as to merit condign punishment, even though permanent excommunication be regarded as too severe a reprisal. Such punishment might well consist in the deprivation of the right to remarry. On this principle a 'guilty' party would be required, in evidence of the reality of his penitence, and as a condition of readmission to communion, not to 'marry' again, at all events during the lifetime of his first partner. Failure to observe this requirement would *ipso facto* render him excommunicate; whilst if he had married a second time *before* showing signs of penitence, he would be permanently debarred from receiving absolution and communion, except perhaps on his death-bed. If this position were adopted, it would provide a rationale for the apparent implications of the 1930 resolution on the question of the 'guilty' party.

Nevertheless, the position is not one which the argument from history endorses. It is of a kind which authority has attempted to enforce more than once in the experience of the Church. Deprivation of the right to marry was one of the disabilities imposed upon penitents in the early centuries : and the rigour of the rule was one of the main reasons why the primitive penitential system collapsed.[1] The same disability was on occasion attached to 'solemn' and even to 'public' penance in the middle ages ; and once again the system proved too rigorous to be capable of enforcement for long.[2] It is beyond the bounds of credibility, therefore, that any attempt to introduce such a penalty in modern conditions could have any real hope of success, at all events if society adopted the view that no greater stigma attached to the remarried 'guilty' than to the remarried 'innocent' party—the view, in fact, which is presupposed by the present state of English law on the subject.

V

Even, therefore, if concessions ought to be made (a question which every man must decide by the verdict of his own conscience), we cannot feel very happy about the form which appears to be given to them by the Lambeth resolutions. If an alternative is to be suggested, it might well be based upon a phrase which occurs with marked emphasis in the report of the 1920 Conference, and was endorsed in 1930.[3] In 1920 the bishops said, 'The Conference affirms as our Lord's principle and

[1] See *The Vision of God*, pp. 228, 275, 506.

[2] See H. C. Lea, *Auricular Confession and Indulgences*, ii, pp. 78–80, 84.

[3] Resolution 67 of 1920; Resolution 11 of 1930.

standard of marriage a life-long and indissoluble union . . . and calls on all Christian people to maintain and bear witness to this standard.' This reminds us at once that the Church has two separate functions. It is at one and the same time a divine organism dispensing grace through sacraments, and a body of people 'witnessing' to certain doctrines and ideals. Consequently it falls naturally into two groups or classes of persons—those who have an official voice in determining the form of the Church's 'witness'; and those who have no official standing, but as individuals have recourse to the Church for the blessings dispensed by God through its ministrations.

It seems reasonable to suggest that all who are officially concerned with the Church's witness to ethical principles should embody those principles in their lives. It seems equally reasonable that to the unofficial members of the Church—those who correspond in effect, though not in fact,[1] to the catechumens of primitive days—the sacraments should be accessible on the most merciful terms compatible with the existence of the Church as an organism at all. If concessions are to be made, they should be made more generously to the unofficial than to the official members of the body; for the latter have publicly accepted a responsibility for 'witnessing' which the former have not, as yet, cared or dared to claim.

[1] The catechumens, of course, were not baptized.

The Church in history has constantly acted upon this principle, in laying more stringent obligations upon the clergy than upon the laity; and curiously enough, the common conscience of to-day, even among Churchmen, assents to it by allowing itself to be surprised, if not shocked, if the clergy indulge in certain forms of relaxation which it regards as wholly innocent for a conscientious layman. But the distinction between 'clergy' and 'laity', though it may in the past have corresponded to our distinction between 'official' and 'unofficial' members of the Church, does so no longer. Since the passing of the Enabling Act there is in existence a lay-hierarchy as clearly defined, in its own way, as the clerical hierarchy. Its ultimate basis is the electoral roll of each separate parish; its lowest step consists of membership of the Parochial Church Council, and its highest pinnacle is membership of the Church Assembly.

The natural course for a Church so constituted, if it genuinely wishes to 'maintain and bear witness' to the standard of indissoluble marriage, would be to insist that no one who violated that standard should be eligible to become, or to remain, a member of this lay-hierarchy: just as we may suppose that wherever possible a bishop withholds his licence from any priest who after divorcing his wife has married another during her lifetime, or who in any circumstances marries a *divorcée* during her first husband's lifetime. The number of laymen and laywomen actually affected by such a provision would be infinitesimally small—as small perhaps as the number of clergy already affected by the withdrawal of the bishop's licence. But a principle of the first importance would have been established—the principle that no one should be allowed any official voice or part (however small) in the organization, administration, supervision, or legislative councils of the Church, who offends against the essential teaching of our Lord about marriage. With such a principle once adopted, the Church could insist that she was giving practical effect to her professions.

What is thus suggested is not a double standard of *conduct*—that dangerous expedient which so often led the Church into difficulties; even though—as I have explained elsewhere—it probably saved Christianity on more than one occasion.[1] It is a double standard of *discipline*, based upon a clear and natural demarcation between those who accept, or desire, official responsibility, and those who do not aspire to it. The latter—the genuine *ecclesia discens* as against the genuine *ecclesia docens* of the two hierarchies—might reasonably expect some concession to their ignorance, doubt, or frailty, such as that embodied in our suggested revision of resolution 11 of Lambeth 1930.[2] For the time perhaps it might be necessary to retain this concession. But if and when the Church became

[1] *The Vision of God*, p. 240. [2] *Supra*, p. 150.

mistress in her own house, it would still be possible to make the experiment of adhering to the rigour of the prohibition of remarriage after divorce in the case of everyone who claimed membership; nor would the further step of reverting to a more merciful attitude towards the unofficial element in the Church be in any way precluded, if the experiment after fair trial proved in the end to be a failure.

In the meantime, it would not seem impossible, even in the Church's present state of bondage, to require all members of the lay-hierarchy to conform to the fundamental principles of the Christian marriage law. There might be difficulties in excluding every person remarried after divorce from the electoral roll; but that would be a small matter. All other 'official' laymen are elected; and therefore all that is needed is that the conscience of Churchmen should be alert to the impropriety of electing anyone who in actual practice has violated that principle of indissoluble marriage to which the Church is bound to witness, either to a Parochial Church Council, or to any higher body. This is merely a matter of consistent and disciplined teaching; and if the bishops at a Lambeth Conference gave a clear lead in the direction suggested, the effect would be electric. On the point of principle there is no open question. Church and State and reason alike agree that marriage is the indissoluble union of one man to one woman, to the exclusion of all others, so long as they both shall live; and that no other form of sex-union is in accordance with the will of God. To state this position, with arguments adapted to modern modes of thought, and answers appropriate to modern questionings, is the primary task of the Church in this matter; and as that task is progressively accomplished, all further obstacles will vanish like the phantoms which in truth they are.

ADDITIONAL NOTE ON S. MATTHEW 19 $^{10-12}$

(*see p.* 68)

FOR convenience of reference this passage can be divided into four sections:

A. 'The disciples say unto him, If the case of the man is so with his wife, it is not expedient to marry.'

B. 'But he said unto them, All men cannot receive this saying, but they to whom it is given.'

C. 'For there are eunuchs, which were so born from their mother's womb; and there are eunuchs, which were made eunuchs by men; and there are eunuchs, which made themselves eunuchs for the kingdom of heaven's sake.'

D. 'He that is able to receive it, let him receive it.'

1. *The relation of the epilogue to the preceding incident.* Whether or no the passage was already attached to the Hillel-Shammai episode from the outset, or was attached to it by Mt. or some intermediate writer (*infra*, 2 (*b*)), its purpose in this position is anything but clear. Everything turns on the meaning of 'this saying' in B. If it refers to the teaching of verses 3–9, the intention is to mitigate its rigour—and it does so with such effect as almost to rob it of all practical value. If on the other hand it refers to the

disciples' comment (A), its purpose is to glorify virginity —as though our Lord were made to say, 'There are indeed good reasons why men should not marry—especially the reason of voluntary celibacy "for the kingdom of heaven's sake". But not everyone is capable of such self-restraint, and therefore it must not be elevated into a universal rule.' There seems little ground for preferring either of these alternatives to the other, except that the latter gives the more natural meaning to the words 'have made themselves eunuchs' (*infra*, 2 (*d*)).

2. *The source and integrity of the passage.*

(*a*) As we have seen (*supra*, p. 70); it was not connected with any of the extant prohibitions of divorce attributed to Jesus, except perhaps that of the Hillel-Shammai incident. If this is its original context we can have little confidence that it emanates from our Lord, for the episode as a whole is quite spurious. But it is highly probable that it did not originally stand even here, for if it did it would have represented the disciples as aghast even at the Shammaite view—i.e., as more lax in outlook than any really serious-minded Jew would countenance.

(*b*) The passage, then, was probably brought into connection, either with the Hillel-Shammai controversy by a writer earlier than S. Matthew, or with the conflated incident (Mt. 19 $^{3-9}$) by S. Matthew himself, for one or other of the purposes mentioned above (*supra*, 1) —in either case the ineptitude of the disciples' dismay being ignored. On this hypothesis, section A is an editorial addition designed to make the bridge between the two passages.

(*c*) We must then consider the source of BCD.

There are several minor possibilities which it is sufficient to enumerate, since they all lead to the same conclusion:—

(i) BCD may have formed a comment upon a lost fragment of teaching, referred to by the words 'this saying'.

(ii) BCD may have existed as a separate logion, the words 'this saying' in B pointing to the central passage C.

(iii) B and D are closely connected both in idea and in language; and make of the whole saying either a 'counsel' or else a piece of 'vocational' morality.[1] Our Lord, as we have seen (*supra*, p. 100), does not seem to have recognized any distinction between 'counsels' and 'precepts', though it is more than once attributed to him by S. Matthew. If, then, B and D imply the doctrine of 'counsels', they are spurious;[2] though C may perfectly well still be genuine. If on the other hand B and D are 'vocational' they add nothing to the saying; for C also is clearly vocational—it praises those ('some') who have 'made themselves eunuchs', without condemning those who have not.

(*d*) In any case, as soon as BCD is recognized as a

[1] The difference between the two can roughly be expressed by saying that a 'counsel' is addressed to all, whatever their way of life, but those who cannot attain to it are excused so long as they keep the 'precepts'; a 'vocational' maxim is addressed only to those who have a special aptitude to the particular way of life to which the maxim applies.

[2] We may add, as an additional reason for treating them as negligible, that D appears to be modelled on 'He that hath ears to hear, let him hear' (Mt. 11 [15], 13 [9, 43]).

saying originally distinct from the divorce tradition, its meaning is obvious. 'Those who have made themselves eunuchs for the kingdom of heaven's sake' are not men who have separated from their wives and refrained from marrying again—a wholly unnatural meaning to get out of the phrase. They are those who have embraced a life of voluntary celibacy. We may still question whether, with this meaning, the saying comes from our Lord's own lips; but the implication is clear. Even if we assume that it was part of a tradition now lost ((*c*) i, above), that tradition was one expressing a call to the celibate life; and if we prefer hypotheses (*c*) ii or iii, the saying by itself upheld the same view.

(*e*) We may add, as before (*supra*, p. 68), that the reference to the 'kingdom' in C cannot mean that the celibate life is regarded as possible only on the understanding that the end of the world is imminent.

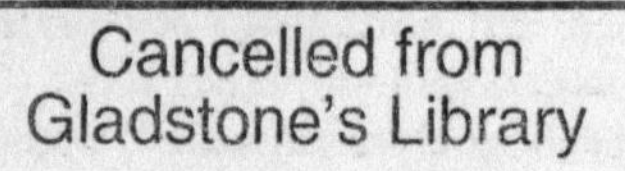

08 MAR 2023

ST. DEINIOL'S LIBRARY,
HAWARDEN.